Engaging Primary Children in Mathematics

Engaging Primary Children in Mathematics

Margaret Sangster

Bloomsbury Academic
An imprint of Bloomsbury Publishing Plc

B L O O M S B U R Y
LONDON · OXFORD · NEW YORK · NEW DELHI · SYDNEY

Bloomsbury Academic

An imprint of Bloomsbury Publishing Plc

50 Bedford Square
London
WC1B 3DP
UK

1385 Broadway
New York
NY 10018
USA

www.bloomsbury.com

**BLOOMSBURY and the Diana logo are trademarks of Bloomsbury
Publishing Plc**

First published 2016

© Margaret Sangster 2016

British Library Cataloguing-in-Publication Data

A catalogue record for this book is available from the British Library.

ISBN:	HB:	978-1-4725-8027-6
	PB:	978-1-4725-8026-9
	ePDF:	978-1-4725-8029-0
	ePub:	978-1-4725-8028-3

Library of Congress Cataloging-in-Publication Data

Sangster, Margaret.
Engaging primary children in mathematics / Margaret Sangster.
pages cm
Includes bibliographical references and index.
ISBN 978-1-4725-8027-6 (hb) — ISBN 978-1-4725-8026-9 (pb) —
ISBN 978-1-4725-8029-0 (epdf) — ISBN 978-1-4725-8028-3 (epub)
1. Mathematics—Study and teaching (Elementary)   I. Title.
QA135.6.S2625 2016
372.7—dc23
2015030728

Typeset by RefineCatch Limited, Bungay, Suffolk
Printed and bound in India

Contents

Part II The Development of the Primary Mathematics Curriculum

Part III Four Key Issues in Learning Primary Mathematics

Preface

Effective teaching is a combination of technical skills, knowledge and beliefs. No where is this more important than in the teaching of mathematics. If teachers understand how children construct their learning they can create an environment where effective learning can take place. This book explores the various strategies for engaging children in mathematical learning in the light of theory and practice. Learning mathematics is not always easy so it is really important to engage children in the subject by giving them the opportunity to experience meaningful mathematics and to use mathematics to explore, create and solve problems.

It is recognized that each teacher has their own way of working based on their beliefs and experience. It is also recognized that there are many structures in place by school and government that must be followed but within those structures there is room for choices. Choices about how teachers explain the mathematics, what type of tasks are set, whether children work together, how their progress is tracked and the resources that are used.

This book examines mathematics teaching and learning in the light of current findings about how the brain constructs, stores, recalls and applies knowledge. There are many excellent books which focus on mathematical content, explaining the intricacies of the curriculum, but here the various elements involved in teaching and learning primary mathematics are drawn together. Each of the topics probably deserves a book of its own but by bringing together the different elements it is hoped that a rationale can be seen for teaching mathematics in particular ways. Mathematical examples are provided where it is useful to illustrate the point being discussed.

Why do you teach mathematics in the way that you do? Although time is a precious commodity in teaching it is always worth taking a little of it to reflect on one's own practice. Hopefully this book will provide some food for thought.

Introduction

The primary teacher's role is to endeavour to give children the confidence to operate in what can be an abstract as well as a tangible world of mathematical ideas, provide a secure foundation of mathematical knowledge and skills and develop an ability to apply known mathematics to new situations. Ideally, by the end of their primary education, children should have a working knowledge of mathematics which they can build on in the future. They should be confident in applying their mathematical knowledge and, if possible, have an enjoyment of the subject.

To achieve this many elements need to be drawn together by the teacher so that an effective learning environment can be created. What do good teachers of mathematics know about how children learn and what strategies do they use to promote the learning of mathematics? By examining some of the issues involved which influence mathematical learning, teachers may reflect on how they teach mathematics in the primary school. Nothing is straightforward in teaching; some issues are ongoing debates such as nature versus nurture and, what comes first, learning the facts or being presented with situations to solve? Teachers will need to make informed decisions about how they approach their teaching. By raising awareness of the influencing factors it is hoped that those decisions will enhance the children's understanding of mathematics.

The elements under review are intertwined but could be considered as three main factors: how children learn, the nature of the mathematics to be learned and the part the teacher plays in that learning.

There are many eminent people who have proposed theories on how children learn; people such as Bruner, Bandura, Piaget and Skinner. All of them have observed the behaviour of children in learning situations. In their time, this was the most accessible way of researching learning. Now we have the technological skill to look inside people's brains. Admittedly it is not yet possible to tell what they are thinking but Magnetic Resonance Imaging (MRI scans) can show how the brain operates when people are presented with images or ideas. This is a revolution in research as it is now possible to begin to link how the brain structures memory to what is being received by the senses.

How can this apply to teaching children mathematics? By studying the mental processes it is possible for the teacher to better tailor the way the mathematics is presented so that it can be retained, recalled and applied. By understanding the way children mentally structure their learning, by understanding what aids effective recall and why children fail to recall particular mathematics it is possible to arrange the mathematics in a way that better enables children to recall and use the mathematics they have experienced.

Mental facility is only one of the factors contributing to learning. Another key factor is the motivation to learn. There are many motivational sources which affect mathematics. Sadly, in England, mathematics often carries with it an image of demotivation as well as motivation. It is difficult to influence external motivation factors such as exams, parents' wishes, competition and league tables but it is possible to foster intrinsic motivation and a desire to engage in mathematics within the classroom. By recognizing the dynamics of self-determination, autonomy and the behaviours that come with self-achievement, the teacher can respond appropriately. Ultimately this can lead to independence. What does an independent mathematician look like (Williams, 2003)? More important, how can the teacher encourage autonomy as opposed to dependency? And, can this be achieved or are there children who remain focussed on performance as opposed to mastery of the subject (Dweck and Elliott, 1988).

At this point attention is turned to the nature of primary mathematics; how it is like a 3D map which builds up over time. How does the teacher manage the progression and interconnectedness of the mathematics? Progression is dealt with well in curricula and text books, connectedness less so (Askew et al., 1997). There is a strong argument to promote the connection of topics based on findings from neurological studies. This is a challenge for linear based schemes and particularly for the teacher faced with these resources. Links across mathematics are often what reveals solutions to problems. A key to functioning as a mathematician is to have an understanding of the relationships which underpin mathematics.

Many children find mathematics difficult, particularly when it moves into more abstract areas where images are not available and progress depends on an understanding of previous knowledge and often a trust in the behaviour of the mathematics. This trust grows out of an understanding of the way numbers and shapes behave. It has been recognized in England that many children were failing mathematics because they were learning methods by rote and then incorrectly remembering the rules. As the rote learning made little sense they could not see the nonsense of their answers. Anita Straker in her government backed Numeracy Project, provided the basis for the Numeracy Strategy (DfEE, 1999), a revolution in England's primary mathematics curriculum.

The Numeracy Strategy offered a curriculum in which there was an emphasis on mental mathematics and a breakdown of calculations into steps which were logical and hopefully understood by children. Probably the move from mental arithmetic tests to discussions of how to work mathematics out in your head has been the most effective move in this new era. The multi-step, extended calculation methods are certainly accessible, but will children move smoothly to more efficient methods which are required by government policy? That is hard to tell. Whatever the result, teachers and children are thinking far more about why mathematics works and that has to be a good thing.

Mathematics moves very quickly into the world of the abstract. In primary school it is still possible to illustrate most of the mathematics by the use of interesting contexts or real life situations. This is advantageous as it enables further neural links to be built which in turn enables recall. Alongside mental mathematics and new calculation approaches, the value of context should be recognized as aiding mathematical learning.

One could argue that there are two topics which receive a disproportionate amount of space in this book. One is calculators and the other is questioning. I feel calculators have received a bad press owing to their unimaginative and limited use and it is important to take this opportunity to revisit their potential contribution to children's mathematical learning. Many task examples are offered to illustrate how they can contribute to children's exploration of number.

Another area which is undervalued is the solving of problems. This can be time consuming and difficult to teach as each problem is different. Problems are often seen as the tag on at the end of a learning sequence. Some children never get to them. They also appear in examinations which in itself could be a justification for their presence in the curriculum. In adult life many experiences of mathematics are in the form of problems which is a stronger justification for their presence. Further, solving a problem is a rewarding and emotionally exciting experience and that is a good reason for their presence. Why learn all that mathematics and not use it?

Some mathematics is difficult, other mathematics is easy. What mathematics do children find difficult? A few examples are unwrapped to show why they are difficult for children to understand. There are also children who find mathematics easy. Maybe they have a natural talent for mathematics? Maybe they just love the subject? Either way, how should the teacher work with these children? Some strategies are suggested that will allow them to have a satisfactory learning experience.

As a final look at the curriculum, patterns, relationships and generalizations are reviewed. Much time is spent learning mathematical facts and calculation methods which, rightly so, are the fundamentals of mathematics but how much time do teachers spend discussing the relationship between numbers, how patterns are structured, how numbers behave in situations and how information can be transferred to new situations? It is this interconnectedness, the linking of roads on the mathematical map, which allows children to transfer their knowledge to new situations and to function as mathematicians.

The third major element of teaching primary mathematics is the teacher. In England, this is usually a 'general' practitioner, the class teacher. The advantage over a specialist is that they know the children in their class well, they can alter the time spent on mathematics and they can allude to mathematics across other subjects. The disadvantage can be the level of confidence in and knowledge they have of the primary mathematics curriculum. The nature of teacher knowledge is considered, from Schulman (1986) through to current thinking about teacher knowledge.

Mathematical knowledge to teach is only one aspect of teaching primary mathematics. There are other aspects to consider such as the kind of learning environment the teacher creates which will include, for example, the displays, the types of task set and the value placed on the contribution of others. Teaching style is unique to each teacher. They have choices about how they set up and run their lessons. Certainly, all teachers work within parameters set by the school, the curriculum and governments but there is lots of 'wriggle room' within lessons. Questioning is a good example of how teachers can encourage thinking in their children and different types of questioning are considered to elicit different types of response. Teachers are in charge of managing the progress of the children through planning and assessing progress and this is briefly addressed, as is the structure of a lesson with a rationale for maintaining certain elements such as mental mathematics, explanations, activities and plenaries.

Teachers can make decisions which promote mathematical learning within their own classrooms but there are decisions made outside the classroom which form the context of teachers' and the children's lives. Teacher's have to recognize these influences and work with them, steering them to their advantage rather than see them as obstacles.

It would be possible to address any one of these topics in greater depth but by bringing these topics together it is hoped to capture the essence of effective mathematics teaching. It is hoped that by collecting them together and justifying the approach you can view how children's mathematics learning can be a more positive and successful experience.

References

Askew, M., Brown, M., Rhodes, V., Wiliam, D. and Johnson, D. (1997) *Effective Teachers of Numeracy: Report of a Study Carried Out for the Teacher Training Agency*, London: King's College London.

Department for Education and Employment (DfEE) (1999) *The National Numeracy Strategy Framework for Teaching Mathematics from Reception to Year 6*, London: DfEE.

Dweck, C. and Elliott, E. (1988) 'A Social-Cognitive Approach to Motivation and Personality' in *Psychological Review*, 95:2, pp. 256–73.

Shulman, L. (1986) 'Those Who Understand: Knowledge Growth in Teaching' in *Educational Researcher*, 15 (February 1986), pp. 4–14.

Williams, J. (2003) *Promoting Independent Learning in the Primary Classroom*, Buckingham: Open University Press.

Part I

How Children Learn Primary Mathematics

1

Constructing Mathematical Knowledge

The neurological story

To enable an understanding of how children learn mathematics it would help to look into the mind and see how it works. Recent advances in neurology have enabled us to be reasonably confident about how the brain is structured and how it functions although we cannot look into the content held in anyone's mind . . . yet!

Very briefly, our human brain has three powerful qualities: plasticity, complexity and capacity. These qualities have enabled us to evolve to lead the complex and sophisticated lives we experience today. The brain is made up of one hundred billion (100,000,000,000) neurons, or brain cells, some of which control subconscious actions and many more collectively form our consciousness or mind. Within our mind we do our thinking which involves such activities as memorizing, communicating, feeling, experiencing emotions, developing spirituality, planning and learning.

Each of the neurons is linked to other neurons through fine threads called dendrites. These are receivers of electrical impulses linked to a chemical reaction. Transmitters called axons connect to the dendrites of other cells at a point called the synapse. At this point there is a chemical reaction allowing the electrical impulse to be passed on, or blocked, if a chemical inhibitor is involved. This is the actual process of thinking – the linking of knowledge held in the neurons. The network developed is massive and efficiently functioning brains can 'fire up' these links almost simultaneously. However, the links must be maintained to survive. If not used, they fade away. One might say, 'use it or lose it'. Interestingly the neurons must be able to retain information as the long-term memory can be 'jogged' back into action so there is the potential for 'reconnection'. This has interesting implications for learning.

A piece of knowledge is stored in a neuron when first learned but to be of any use it must be linked to other neurons through the maintenance of the

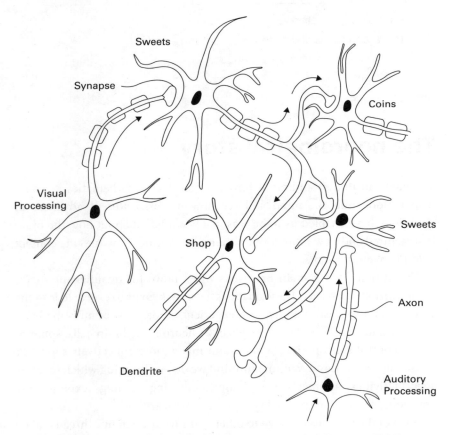

Figure 1 Neurons, axons and synapses (adapted from Barnes, 2007)

axons. The more links made to other pieces of knowledge the more likely it will be 'useable'. This also predisposes that prior associated knowledge will be useful in establishing new knowledge. Further, frequent visits (rehearsals) to that knowledge will maintain it in memory.

Therefore, in teaching mathematics, the implications would be that it is good to build up children's knowledge by linking it to mathematics already learned and for the teacher and pupil to make reference to prior learning. It would also indicate that experiencing the mathematics in different ways is more likely to make it neurologically 'secure' as there will be many links to be called upon. And, that revisiting the mathematics will ensure the neurological links are maintained and not lost.

As adults, it is likely that you have experienced all three of these 'mind' situations. Firstly, how much easier it is to learn (understand) something new when we liken it to something we already know. Secondly, that if we have experienced something in many different situations it becomes familiar and we are able to rapidly realize what is needed. Thirdly, how using a piece of knowledge or a skill frequently allows us to respond quickly and confidently. Why should it be any different for children learning mathematics?

Neurological awareness is important in mathematics because mathematical learning often builds on prior knowledge. For example, learning how to do division depends on prior knowledge of multiplication tables and remainders. Experience of division in a variety of problem solving contexts helps to recognize it is required in new problems and regular visits to doing division keeps the skill and knowledge fresh in the mind and ready to use. Even simple knowledge such as counting goes through the same mental process and certainly using formulae require a 'use it' approach. If not used, we have to cast around for other links to recall knowledge or we have to relearn the mathematics.

For the above reasons, building a strong network of mathematical understanding is crucial to children's mathematical progress.

Is there an innate ability to learn mathematics?

This is a question that often arises when you hear parents at parents' evening saying, 'Well, I was no good at maths at school so I am not surprised she is no good either'. The implication of this comment being it is a hereditary inability and therefore must be in the genes. Likewise, there are families where strong mathematical ability seems to pass down through the generations. One of the great ongoing debates is how much successful learning is the result of genes and how much the environment one is exposed to – we have all heard of the 'nature versus nurture' argument. Of course, it is very difficult to prove because we all have different experiences as we grow up and on the way are devising different neural networks. There is no doubt that both genes and environment play a part in our make-up so now it is a question of where the balance lies. Whichever way the argument currently flows, it is important to expect children to meet the challenges of mathematics and not assume they are not capable of doing it. To have low expectations of a child is doing them a great disservice.

A poor performance by a child could be down to missing prior knowledge. What has been their learning experience to date? Were they absent from school when this topic was taught? It could be that learning has not been effectively organized in the learner's mind – they are muddled about aspects of the mathematics and need specific help to sort it out. It could be that they struggle to recall information because they have few established links in their mind. This might be as a result of not seeing the relationship to prior knowledge or insufficient visits to practise the mathematics or learning in a context which has no meaning for them.

However, there is evidence of a belief in varying natural ability (nature) and teachers will recognize that some children are more able than others to grasp quickly mathematical ideas. LePine et al. (2000) draw upon several sources to explain what might be happening in the brain:

> Those with higher levels of g [cognitive ability] are able to represent more information in the cognitive space where the data that guide behaviour are processed (i.e., working memory). As a result, those with higher levels of g are able to learn more quickly from their experiences and are able to develop larger and more efficiently organized stores of job knowledge and skills.
>
> LePine et al., p. 567

From observation, Howard Gardner built a theoretical model (Gardner, 1983) which identified seven areas of ability which people have in different amounts. His original abilities were, mathematical, musical, spatial, linguistic, logical, kinaesthetic and personal. These are not found in separate areas of the brain but function across the cortex, tapping into a particular set of neurons. Since then he has developed his theory and in 1999 his list read:

linguistic, logical mathematical, spatial, bodily kinaesthetic, musical, naturalist, intra-personal, interpersonal and existential (Gardner, 1999). Everyone's mind is unique and will be a mix of all these abilities. His theory, based on research of patients with head injuries, is enticing and seems to confirm observations of performance but all adults have been exposed extensively to environmental factors and have had many years to build up their neural networks so would the same be true for children? One could reason that if similar neural patterns occur in many adults there is a strong possibility that human minds do organize themselves in similar ways and therefore his ideas are relevant to children.

Whether nature or nurture, both play a part in children's learning of mathematics. The teacher's role is to set up the most effective learning environment that he or she can and, as far as possible, recognize the mathematical needs of the individuals within it.

Effective learning of mathematics

There are too many theories about how children learn to mention them all here. I have selected one or two which appear to support the emerging neurological evidence prior to the information revealed by scanning the brain. Most noted of these is the work of Jean Piaget, a psychologist, who between 1920 and 1980 made extensive observations of children carrying out tasks, on which he built several theories about learning. He suggested that children built up 'schemata' in their brain which were units of knowledge and processes which were linked. (An early view of neural networks?) His ideas on 'assimilation' and 'accommodation' (Piaget, 1952) sit well with current scientific enquiries too. Assimilation is the adaptation of existing schemata to take on new knowledge (attaching it to prior learning) and accommodation is when current knowledge needs to be changed to fit with the new learning. For example, assimilation would occur when a child learns that shapes with three straight sides are called triangles. Accommodation would occur when the child finds out that not all triangles have horizontal bases.

Richard Skemp, in his book *The Psychology of Learning Mathematics* (1971), describes two types of learning, 'instrumental' and 'relational'. Instrumental learning takes place when children are learning facts and formulae and routines. They are reproduced word for word in the required situation rather like learning spellings. These are essential pieces of knowledge. The relational aspect of mathematics, according to Skemp, occurs when children apply their mathematics in situations where they are required to think and work out solutions. This could well be a description of children drawing upon their neural links to resolve a situation and possibly create new ones.

Another way of looking at how children learn was offered by Robert Nola in 1997. He talks about 'knowing' which is defined by observing how a person responds to a situation and it implies the depth of their understanding or maybe their type of understanding? He offers six types of knowing:

1   A person knows a direct object
2   A person knows how to do something
3   A person knows how to explain
4   A person knows why something works
5   A person knows that something happens
6   A person knows what something is.

Based on Nola (1997), p. 62

Type 1 could be described as knowing directly that the symbol 6 represents the number six or represents six objects or follows 5 in the counting rhyme. Another example would be to know that 6 × 9 is 54 without having to work anything out. One might describe these as learned facts. The second type, knowing how to do something, could be a method or a skill, for example, knowing a rhyme for doing subtraction calculations or constructing an equilateral triangle. Type 6 is the recognition and labelling of a situation. Types 1, 2 and 6 are closely matched to Skemp's instrumental learning. One could argue that types 1 and 2 cover the core knowledge that all primary children should have.

Type 3 is interesting as it requires children to articulate what they are experiencing. This draws upon an ability to use language which may not be required to any extent in other mathematical situations. Type 4 takes this one step further in expecting an explanation of why it works. Taken together, an example of this would be the difference between saying all the numbers move one place to the left when multiplying by ten and expecting a child to explain that this happens because each column is ten times greater than the column to its right (the intrinsic structure of the decimal system).

Type 5 is particularly interesting as it implies a degree of prediction underpinned by a sense of how mathematics behaves. A simple example would be knowing that ten more than a number will always have the same unit digit. A more challenging example would be that, if two angles of a triangle are 20° and 30°, the third angle will always be 130°. Types 4 and 5 and to some extent type 3 require children to have an understanding of the mathematics. It could be argued that this kind of understanding will enable children to build a more complex and flexible mental network which, in turn, will allow them to function more effectively as mathematicians. The danger would be to assume that if the facts are learned first, the thinking can come later. Setting up contexts in which the facts exist but thinking is required, as well as challenges to apply mathematics, will create stronger neural networks which, in turn, can be called upon in a variety of ways in new situations.

It would be wrong to leave this chapter without referring to two other factors which influence the brain when learning; 'social' and 'emotional' influences. Social construction theory is based on the premise that humans are social beings and therefore are more effective learners when working with others. If oral expression and aural input strengthens a child's ability to learn then a social learning approach could be effective. Also, if children are able to work together and draw upon the group's knowledge this too will have its advantages. Classroom experience indicates there is a mixture of preferred learning styles with some children benefiting from working together and some children who prefer to work on their own. The teacher will need to decide which is appropriate and when. In the future, as adults, the skill of working in teams and alone will both be required.

Emotional factors are increasingly being seen as having an effect on children's learning. Barnes calls upon the work of Damasio (2003: 35) to promote the idea of 'well-ness' and 'well-being' and as a consequence a state in which optimum learning can take place. Applying this to the classroom Barnes (2007) suggests that it is important for teachers to provide:

- a comfortable and warm place where basic physical needs are supplied
- a place where positive experience for each individual is more likely than negative experience
- a curricular concentration on promoting conditions of well-being
- a close knowledge of the lives of the children beyond the classroom.

Barnes, p. 88

It is fascinating to realize that close observation by people such as Piaget and Skemp enabled them to develop models of learning that are being confirmed by recent scientific experiments. It is exciting to learn about recent discoveries in neurology but it is important to reflect on how this might affect our approach to teaching mathematics. Many of the actions that teacher's take in the classroom are confirmed by the findings discussed in this chapter but there might be some here which will influence the way you work with children. In teaching mathematics a key question to ask is whether we achieve the right balance of learning facts and procedures with opportunities to apply the mathematics in a variety of contexts and thus strengthen the neural networks around and between topics.

References

Barnes, J. (2007) *Cross-Curricular Learning 3–14*, London: Paul Chapman Publishing.

Damasio, A. (2003) *Looking for Spinoza: Joy, Sorrow and the Feeling Brain*, Orlando, FL: Harcourt.

Gardner, H. (1983) *Frames of Mind: A Theory of Multiple Intelligences*, London: Heineman.

Gardner, H. (1999) *Intelligence Reframed: Multiple Intelligence for the 21st century*, New York: Basic Books.

LePine, J., Colquitt, J. and Erez, A. (2000) 'Adaptability to Changing Task Contexts: Effects of General Cognitive Ability, Conscientiousness and Openness to Experience' in *Personnel Psychology*, 53, pp. 563–93.

Nola, R. (1997) 'Constructivism in Science and Science Education: A Philosophical Critique' in *Science and Education*, 6, 1–2, pp. 55–83.

Piaget, J. (1952) (translated by M. Cook) *The Origins of Intelligence in Children*, New York: International Universities Press.

Skemp, R. (1971) *The Psychology of Learning Mathematics*, London: Penguin.

2

Recalling and Transferring Mathematical Knowledge

Mathematics is seen as an essential qualification in exam-orientated cultures and many students are successful because they have learned a set of facts and a set of processes. They hope to recognize the mathematics in sufficient questions to pass the exam. It would be fair to say that many students have little sense of being a mathematician or having a feel for the subject. In some ways this is the 'bottom line' in mathematical success. It is worth considering what is happening here to see if we can make mathematics more engaging.

Initially children are presented with a new mathematics topic. If it is unrelated to anything they have done before they will establish a memory of the experience. If it is connected to previous knowledge more neural links will be made. These links are important when it comes to retrieving the knowledge.

> Generally, the number of future retrieval routes available for students is in proportion to the number of meaningful connections generated by them. In other words, the greater the number of similarities or analogical relationships that can be identified between past and present and future situations, the easier it will be for significant transfer of learning to occur.

Calais (2006: 7)

This is reflected in the Kings College findings that 'connectionist' teachers have more success (Askew et al., 1997). Although it was a small study, they found that if teachers linked new work to knowledge already gained, the children would do better. This could be helped by reminding children of past mathematics that they can build on when new topics are introduced; 'Do you remember when . . .' and providing work in a range of contexts enabling more neural links to be made. If we accept what Calais is saying, and there is strong neural evidence to suggest it is true, then experience of applying mathematics is well justified.

For children to be able to recall information it needs to enter the long-term memory. On first contact with the mathematics it enters the short-term memory and it is believed that it rapidly moves to the long-term memory. What is stored may be an image or words or actions. When words are available, more sophisticated understanding can be achieved as the abstract can be described and mathematics which can not be created in a memorable image can be stored verbally in the memory (Vygotsky, 1934/91). The crucial point comes when a child revisits the mathematics, whether it is the next day or the next week or even the next year. The knowledge or skill has to be retrieved. This depends on the child linking what is in front of them to the knowledge in their memory. If the neural pathway is singular or the understanding only known to apply to a single situation, then the child will only respond if the situation is identical. For example, a child might be successful in recalling $3 \times 4 = 12$ but struggle when asked how many cakes are needed to place 4 cakes on each of 3 plates. We see this difficulty with children who have not established the understanding that this mathematics can be applied in different situations. Recall of facts such as tables does not require application so can be purely a memory task. As soon as a child is asked to apply his or her knowledge, then the situation has to be assessed and knowledge selected. Another really early example is, 'What number comes before 6?' The child has to recall the counting rhyme and then select the number 5 either by recounting and remembering what was said before 6 or by using a backward counting rhyme but will later know it is 5 because they have built up a stronger experience of the counting rhyme.

A more challenging example is the word problem where a child has to decide what mathematics to use. For example, in a toy factory the packer had to fill a large box of dimensions 36 cm by 24 cm by 96 cm with smaller boxes of 3 cm by 4 cm by 8 cm. How many small boxes could the packer fit in the large box? This is a multi-step problem. First, how can the information be sorted so that a way forward can be established? Second, what mathematics should be used here? Third, doing the calculations and finally, checking to see if the answer is reasonable or correct. Possibly the hardest part of this problem is recognizing the mathematics needed. Maybe the child has met a similar problem before. Maybe they are secure in their understanding of volume and measuring cuboids. Both will help them get started. Both rely on prior knowledge. If the problem is met immediately after doing work in these areas a child will be more successful. If the problem is met in a one-off situation such as an exam the success rate will fall as they have less chance of selecting the appropriate memory.

How can we help children recall and apply knowledge in new situations?

Some facts need to be known. They are like vocabulary which allows expression of ideas. Whereas one learns spellings, one can learn number facts. This is seen when children rehearse the counting rhyme, the even number sequence, calculation routines, tables and formulae such as 'length times breadth equals area' (of a rectangle). This is useful knowledge to have but it is meaningless unless it is applied. Learning a chant is totally oral and aural. With an image attached it offers a visual memory and with explanation and discussion it can offer further meaning and therefore greater understanding. As well as a multi-sensory approach, offering situations for children to apply the knowledge is crucial to establishing more neural links and hence having a better chance of useful recall. The topic of Measure is a good example of where a practical skill application approach can be taken.

Sometimes children are so busy doing practices that they completely miss the relational aspect of the mathematics. For example, a child might fill in a whole page of additions, diligently using cubes to find each answer and not realize that many of the calculations are reversals of previous ones (3 + 4 and 4 + 3), They completely miss the point that addition is commutative. The principle of commutativity is the key point; the mathematics that will be useful later; the mathematics that needs to be recognized in new situations. This is what Skemp (1976) means by relational mathematics – the understanding behind the immediate actions. As teachers, we can help children with this by identifying it as a teaching point, discussing the principle with the children and reiterating it at the end of the lesson in the plenary/summary.

Increasing the neural links by providing a variety of situations to apply the mathematics is one way of strengthening recall and application but also discussing the process of entering and doing the mathematics will help. Like the Hungarian approach to homework (Andrews and Hatch, 2005), talking in depth about one example is probably better than doing twenty examples without considering how the mathematics was done and why it works.

In England, a while ago, mathematics was often something you worked at from a book, in silence, taking a completed page to the teacher to be marked before moving on to the next page. The Numeracy Strategy (DfEE, 1999) recognized the important role of the teacher in talking to the class about the mathematics they were doing. Maybe the potential of children working together on mathematics has not yet been fully realized. There is a genuine concern that some children will copy without understanding and that some will become dependent on other children. Consider though, does copying come from laziness or a lack of understanding and/or a desperate need to keep up with the rest of the class? It is not easy to get children to recognize their own needs and declare them but if an environment can be created where such discussions are open and respected the children will become more engaged in their own learning.

Transfer (and generalization)

A key element of doing mathematics is the ability to transfer knowledge to new situations. Practising and applying mathematics supports memory and recall but mathematics is more than this. Children need to be able to bring old knowledge to new situations, sometimes to adapt it and sometimes create new knowledge. Transfer and generalization are vital processes if children are to be successful mathematicians.

Mathematics in the early years is real, practical and concrete, or is it? True, children learn to count using objects and begin adding and subtracting by moving objects. But the counting rhyme is an invention by man, the numerals are symbols that do not exist in the natural world and calculations are methods invented by humans. And so, children meet their first layer of abstraction – the number system. They need to understand that numbers behave consistently such as 6 always follows 5, 3 + 5 is always 8 and 10 − 4 is always 6. They also need to understand that the number system can be applied to different objects and in different situations; 7 dinosaurs today, could be 7 apples tomorrow and 7 people on the next day. Here we already have two fundamental principles of an abstract nature and we have only just started counting, adding and subtracting simple numbers!

All mathematics has a degree of generality if it is to be transferred to new situations. Children need to realize that 'old' mathematics can be applied in 'new' situations otherwise it is of no use. Many low attainers find this transfer difficult because they do not understand the principle of transfer and have not yet developed a sense of mathematical generality. I have witnessed children who have visited counting one day and when they are given different objects to count the next day it is as if they are learning to count all over again. No connection is made with the previous day's counting because the context has changed. Transfer is not yet taking place. Further on in the curriculum as children move towards a study of relationships and algebra Mason et al. (1985: 46) remark:

> Generalized arithmetic can prove a difficult route by itself, since it is an abstraction of an already abstract idea. Nevertheless, this is the route most favoured in school texts.

I would argue that the first stage of generalization begins as soon as children enter the world of mathematics. Transfer of mathematical principles and knowledge lie at the heart of mathematical success. Many children become proficient at the manipulation of numerical symbols as these form a prominent aspect of routine teaching but then find difficulty in transferring these calculation methods to questions which involve words. Looking more closely at the mental process of transfer, Calais (2006: 2) states:

> Since virtually all learning entails connecting past learning to new situations, all transfer, therefore, entails transfer of learning. However, because nothing ever recurs in exactly identical ways or in exactly identical contexts, the fundamental problem in transfer involves perceiving when and how something is identical to or equivalent to something else.

He goes on to summarize Haskell's taxonomy of Levels of Transfer (2001) to which I have added examples from primary mathematics:

Level 1 Non-specific transfer – all learning is transfer because the mind recalls prior learning, e.g. reciting tables or number facts.

Level 2 Application transfer – applying counting to another counting situation.

Level 3 Context transfer – seeing a similar mathematical situation to a previous one and selecting the same method. E.g. measuring the area of a shape.

Level 4 Near transfer – new learning occurs close to what is already known such as counting squares to find the area of a shape and now tackling an irregular shape.

Level 5 Far transfer – new learning occurs in situations far removed from the one in which it was learned; e.g. choosing to use a graph to show results in a science experiment when graphs have not been studied recently so there is no clue present as to what mathematics to apply.

Level 6 Displacement or creative transfer – the learner connects two remote situations and creates for them a new concept; e.g. the learner discovers a link between area and the volume of cuboids which they had not known before.

Whilst one may see some overlap in these categories, Haskell's taxonomy takes us through the learner's experience from the simplicity of everyday learning to the complexity of discovering or creating new knowledge which may be experienced by a child venturing into new territory.

Results of testing, nationally and internationally, indicate that children are less successful at applying knowledge than calculating. As this Ofsted report (2008) shows:

> Achievement and standards in 'using and applying mathematics' remains lower than in other areas of mathematics. These higher order skills underpin what it means to behave mathematically. It is of serious concern, therefore, that national tests do not require pupils to use and apply mathematics in substantial tasks through which they are able to decide what approaches to adopt, use a range of mathematical techniques in exploring the problem, find solutions, generalise and communicate their reasoning.
>
> Ofsted, point 91, p. 35

Such situations require correct identification of the mathematics and successful transfer of knowledge. Bodner (2000) suggests that unsuccessful problem solvers construct initial representations that activate inappropriate schema for the problem. Such action results in either a lack of relevant information being called to mind or inappropriate strategies/calculations being applied. Generally there is a failure to understand the problem and its context. Children are easily thrown by unfamiliar contexts. For example, one of the early English national test papers for seven-year-olds set a series of questions around the theme of a fairground. How many seven-year-olds have been to a fairground?

Mathematics is an abstract subject applied to tangible situations. This is the first step in generalization but realizing the underlying principles is as important as the task being completed. Understanding the principles and sufficient prior experience are the essence of successful transfer to new situations. Sometimes it is easier to learn the rule rather than explain what is happening but if explained, the mathematics is exposed. See the box Dividing fractions by fractions for an example.

Dividing fractions by fractions

1/8 divided by 1/4

This can be done by learning the rule of turning the second fraction over and multiplying along the top and along the bottom and then cancelling:

$$\frac{1}{8} \times \frac{4}{1} = \frac{4}{8} = \frac{1}{2}$$

But then you might ask why, if you are dividing, you get a bigger answer than either of the numbers you started with?

Maybe children could look at the following sequence:

Picture a bar of chocolate:

4 bars divided by 1 = 4 bars (How many times does 1 fit into 4?)

1 bar divided by 1/4 = 4 pieces (How many times does 1/4 fit into 1?)

1/2 bar divided by 1/4 = 2 pieces (How many times does a 1/4 fit into a half?)

1/4 bar divided by 1/4 = 1 piece (How many times does 1/4 fit into 1/4?)

1/8 divided by 1/4 = 1/2 a piece (How many times does a 1/4 fit into 1/8? It doesn't, only 1/2 of it will fit in.)

Sometimes it is about finding the right words to create a logical image. Sometimes words will not describe the mathematical relationship and we have to accept what the numbers are saying.

Generalization will be considered more closely in Chapter 13 when patterns and relationships are discussed. Having looked more closely at recall and transfer and the nature of mathematics itself, we can see the complexity of the subject and what children need to be experiencing and thinking when they learn mathematics so that they are able to transfer their knowledge to new situations, in fact, so that they can operate as emergent mathematicians.

References

Andrews, P. and Hatch, G. (2005) 'Hungary and its Characteristic Pedagogic Flow' in *Proceedings of the British Society for Research into Learning Mathematics* (BSRLM), 21:2 (July 2001), pp. 26–40.

Askew, M., Brown, M., Rhodes, V., Wiliam, D. and Johnson, D. (1997) *Effective Teachers of Numeracy in Primary Schools: Teachers' Beliefs, Practices and Pupils' Learning*, London: Kings College London.

Bodner, G. (2000) 'Mental Models: The Role of Representations in Problem Solving in Chemistry', *University Chemistry Education*, 4: 24–30.

Calais, G. (2006) 'Haskell's Taxonomies of Transfer of Learning: Implications for Classroom Instruction' in *National Forum of Applied Educational Research Journal*, 20:3, pp. 1–8.

Department for Education and Employment (DfEE) (1999) *The National Numeracy Strategy: Framework for Teaching Mathematics from Reception to Year 6*, London: DfEE.

Haskell, E. (2001) *Transfer of Learning: Cognition, Instruction, and Reasoning*, New York: Academic Press cited in G. Calais (2006) 'Haskell's Taxonomies of Transfer of Learning: Implications for Classroom Instruction' in *National Forum of Applied Educational Research Journal*, 20:3, pp. 1–8.

Mason, J., Pimm, D., Graham, A. and Gowar, N. (1985) *Routes to/Roots of Algebra*, Milton Keynes: Open University Press.

Office for Standards in Education (Ofsted) (2008) *Mathematics: Understanding the Score*, Reference no. 070063, London: Ofsted.

Skemp, R. (1976) 'Relational Understanding and Instrumental Understanding', in *Mathematics Teaching*, 77, pp. 20–6.

Vygotsky, L. (1934/1991) *Thought and Language* (1991 translation by Kozulin), Cambridge, MA: MIT Press.

3

Desirable Outcomes and Motivations

Desirable outcomes in mathematics are what people wish to achieve either for themselves or for others. Motivation provides the willingness to engage in the mathematics and motivators can be internal or external. For children to be internally motivated is prized in education as it is likely to result in sustained and effective learning but external motivators can also be very powerful in the short term.

External pressures

Mathematics alongside first language study are the two fundamental qualifications that employers seek. To function in the workplace these qualifications underpin most other skills that are required. And yet, achieving a basic national qualification in mathematics at the age of sixteen (England) has proved quite difficult for a large number of students. Despite this, students who need the qualification to progress are willing to persevere in their studies, hopeful of a successful outcome. Need is a strong motivator for those who wish to gain a qualification. Interestingly, those who use mathematics in the workplace usually become very adept in the required aspect with or without a qualification. Consider how much arithmetic builders, plumbers, dressmakers and accountants use. Experience, with its repeated calculations, establishes strong neural pathways.

Parents are often a source of external motivation. They are usually keen for their children to progress and therefore emit messages about the importance of gaining mathematics qualifications. Sometimes these messages are mixed. Some parents will help their children with mathematics homework whilst declaring they were no good at maths at school, giving the impression of low expectation for their children. This is unfortunate and rather dilutes the messages about expectation. Sadly, a few parents take no interest in their child's education which can be quite demotivating. Contrast with this the parent who pays for additional coaching in mathematics for their child. As with all attitudes, there is a middle road of supportive parents, willing to assist their children where they can.

Interestingly, in a study by Grolnick and Ryan (1989: 338) in America, parents who encouraged their children to be more independent but were also involved in their children's education had children who were more intrinsically motivated and who performed better in school than those who were more controlling and less involved. This suggests that showing interest but also encouraging children to make decisions leads to higher achievement.

Schools in England and many other countries now exist in a world where accountability is a priority. Through inspections, exam results and league tables schools' performances are measured and there are consequences if they do not reach the expected performance level. Here, the governments are exerting a form of external motivation on the school to do well. This pressure is felt by children through the behaviour of the teachers, the school and possibly the parents.

It is the teacher who has to ensure the progress of the children in his or her class. In mathematics this is done in several ways: through good teaching, through testing nationally and at school level, through individual coaching and through 'delivering' the required curriculum. Teachers have direct external motivators as they are observed and graded in inspections and their class' results analysed and action plans drawn up. Although not discussed with children, the external pressures on the teacher are present in many of their actions in the classroom. In a 1981 research study by Deci et al. (1991: 340) they found that teachers under pressure are likely to respond by adopting a controlling approach with their class. A further study by Flink et al. in 1990 confirmed their findings and additionally found that the teachers who exerted more control had students who performed less well in problem solving.

Last, but not least, is the motivation of the child. Clearly they are subject to the attitudes and pressures of all the above interested parties but they also will have their own motivations. Do they respond to the pressure of others? Do they value the wishes of those around them? Do they like mathematics and enjoy taking part in mathematics lessons? Are they successful and motivated by achievement? Do they like mathematics because they work with other children? What actually motivates individuals?

Motivation

Motivation is an issue in mathematics learning, more so with older children than those in the primary school. Some of this can be put down to the abstract and difficult nature of the subject, but not entirely. By more closely examining the influences in the classroom on children's motivation it is possible to consider ways to increase children's engagement with mathematics. There have been some significant studies over the last thirty years, mainly in America, about how children respond to situations. If we accept that independent working, or autonomy, is a good learning mode then it would be valid to develop this quality in children. Deci and Ryan (1985) describe a spectrum of self-determination ranging from 'external' motivation, through 'introjected' and 'identified' to 'integrated' motivation where the child has moved from having to do what they are told, gradually recognizing the value of the rules until they reach the point where they adopt the rules as their own and it becomes part of the values underpinning their work approach. Grolnick and Ryan in 1989 go on to show that: '[I]nternalization will proceed most effectively toward self-determined forms of regulation if (a) children understand the personal utility of the activity, (b) they are provided choices about the activity with a minimum of pressure, and (c) their feelings and perspective are acknowledged.' (1989: 338). So here we begin to see aspects that might assist in the engagement of mathematics, mathematics which contains a sense of reality and purpose, choices around the activities to be completed and discussion about the mathematics and way of working.

One cannot consider the role of motivation in children's learning without referring to the extensive work of Carol Dweck. From her studies in the

1980s through to the present day she has made a close examination of children's responses to tasks. She has categorized children's motivational behaviour into two major groups; those children who have 'performance orientated goals' and those who have 'mastery orientated goals'. We would recognize performance orientated children as those who feel good about finishing the task and getting rewarded and mastery orientated children as those who strive to master a skill, are interested in solving the problem because it is interesting and are generally keen to improve their skills and knowledge rather than just finish the task and gain approval/reward. Most importantly, these are the children whom she found progressed further because they were willing to take on the challenge and accepted failure and renewed attempts as part of the learning process. One might say these children had greater internal motivation but we cannot know this from observation only.

One of her studies (Dweck and Elliott, 1988) involved 100 eleven-year-olds who were asked to complete increasingly difficult pattern recognition tasks. When performance achievement goals were presented to children who believed they had low ability they attributed their failures to their lack of ability and often gave up. Dweck labelled this response 'learned helplessness'. In contrast, those who believed in their own ability and the goal was to master the task persevered even when experiencing initial failure. Interestingly the able performance orientated children avoided the harder tasks possibly because they risked public failure. As you can imagine, the mastery orientated children progressed more rapidly. The 'helpless' children displayed pronounced negative behaviours:

> Specifically, they reported such things as an aversion to the task, boredom with the problems, or anxiety over their performance ... more than two-thirds of the helpless children (but virtually none of the mastery-oriented ones) engaged in task-irrelevant verbalizations, usually of diversionary or self-aggrandizing nature. For example, some attempted to alter the rules of the task, some spoke of talents in other domains, and some boasted of unusual wealth and possessions, presumably in an attempt to direct attention away from their present performance and toward more successful endeavors or praiseworthy attributes.
>
> Dweck and Elliott (1988), p. 6

I think we all recognize these diversionary tactics which Dweck saw as children's attempts to bolster their own image and confidence. Mathematics is particularly vulnerable to a performance goal approach. Tasks generally increase in difficulty, many are happy to confess to failure, there is a strong culture of reward as opposed to celebrating the journey and the effort and, the 'task and tick' culture continues to dominate many classrooms. Is it possible to turn mathematics learning into a mastery orientated subject so that children can become that kind of learner? The National Numeracy Strategy (DfEE, 1999) approach in England has offered opportunities for children to engage in discussion of the 'how' of mathematics which can only be a good move toward 'mastery'.

Since Dweck's work, the motivation path has twisted again. In challenging the theory that a mastery approach is more effective in the long term and drawing upon the work of Huang (2011) who suggested both mastery and performance goals benefit achievement, Seaton et al. (2014) set up a study with 2,786 secondary school students (aged eleven to seventeen) in Australia. They found that the link between a mastery orientated approach and achievement was weak, but self-concept (a Marsh and Craven, 2006 term) in mathematical achievement was a stronger predictor of actual achievement. They also found that performance goal orientation predicted subsequent mathematical success. This agreed with Durick et al.'s findings (2009) but not with Paulick et al.'s (2013). This was possibly due to the fact that it was a general subject study and was with early secondary school students (eleven to twelve years old). This may be an indicator that performance goal orientation increases in the teenage years. The most marked findings of Seaton et al.'s study is the importance of the role of self-concept or confidence in one's own mathematical ability that was the greatest influencing factor. This is a factor worth considering for primary pupils too.

Engaging children in mathematics

All classrooms and teachers are different and the factors which affect learning are various. It is important to consider how the student feels about their own learning as much as it is about the teacher's focus on what is important. Therefore, what helps?

Based on the findings of Dweck we should be seeking to create a mastery orientated classroom. Ames (1992: 262) describes this as one which is 'focussed on understanding content and mastering new skills [with] a willingness to engage in the learning process'. It is important for children to believe that effort leads to success and children derive satisfaction from being successful in the task rather than doing the task solely for the reward. However, if we agree with Deci and Ryan's spectrum of autonomy (1985) it might be necessary to begin with external reward and gradually work towards an internalized self-determination or autonomy. The danger is to stay on the external reward structure and not move along the spectrum. This is quite understandable as all teachers seek control of the children in their class.

Control has come under the spotlight too. Ames sees controlling behaviour through reward and external inducements as increasing skills and self-perception in the short term but not the independence of long-term development enhanced by intrinsic motivation. In fact Ryan and Connell (1989) found that controlling teachers created greater anxiety in their pupils and difficulties in coping with failure. This was noted earlier by Deci et al. (1981, cited in Deci et al., 1991: 337): '[T]eachers' orientations influence the general classroom climate, and the results revealed that students in classrooms with autonomy supportive teachers displayed more intrinsic motivation, perceived competence, and self-esteem than did students in classrooms with controlling teachers.'

Generally, it is believed that if a teacher wants to create independent, autonomous learners there needs to be the opportunity for them to self-manage some of their learning. This can be done through giving them choices about tasks and time for completion, by discussing the content of the tasks rather than just acknowledging the completion of the task; by rewarding effort as well as accomplishment and by providing meaningful and engaging contexts in which to learn. Too much praise can lead to dependency and is re-enforcing external motivation. There is a fine line to tread and it will vary from child to child. Who is ready for more autonomy? As Dweck says in her YouTube presentation (accessed 2011): 'We should not praise things which are easy, require little effort, is flawless first go, and should not expose deficiency. . . . We should value thinking things through, taking on something hard, asking what should we do when stuck.'

Finally, if children feel secure and confident in their classroom setting and within their mathematics they are more likely to progress. This security can come from several directions: the teacher's responses to their work, the relationship they have with their peers both in working together and speaking out in front of others and, in the attitude taken by the other adults in their lives. Do children feel they 'belong' in your mathematics lessons and can they 'contribute'?

What do we desire of our children's education; the compliant or the challenging, the dependent or the autonomous child; or all of these at different times. It is complex but it is also a journey towards a functioning, engaged adult. By consciously reflecting on our actions and promoting particular strategies as teachers can we move the children in their mathematics to engaged, autonomous learners? Guy Claxton (2007: 1) quoted Sir Richard Livingstone (1941), 'The test of successful education is not the amount of knowledge that pupils take away from school, but their appetite to know and their *capacity to learn*.'

References

Ames, C. (1992) 'Classrooms: Goals, Structures and Student Motivation' in *Journal of Educational Psychologist*, 84:3, pp. 261–71.

Claxton, G. (2007) 'Expanding Young People's Capacity to Learn' in *British Journal of Educational Studies*, June 2007, pp. 1–20.

Deci, E. and Ryan, R. (1985) *Intrinsic Motivation and Self-Determination in Human Behavior*, New York: Plenum, cited in E. Deci, R. Vallerand, L. Pelletier and R. Ryan (1991), 'Motivation and Education: The Self-Determination Perspective' in *Educational Psychologist*, 26:3/4, pp. 325–46.

Deci, E., Schwartz, A., Sheinman, L. and Ryan, R. (1981) 'An Instrument to Assess Adults' Orientation Toward Control Versus Autonomy with Children: Reflections on Intrinsic Motivation and Perceived Competence' in *Journal of Educational Psychology*, 73 (pp. 642–50), cited in E. Deci, R. Vallerand, L. Pelletier and R. Ryan (1991), 'Motivation and Education: The Self-Determination Perspective' in *Educational Psychologist*, 26:3/4, pp. 325–46.

Department for Education and Employment (DfEE) (1999) *The National Numeracy Strategy Framework for Teaching Mathematics from Reception to Year 6*, London: DfEE.

Durick, A., Lovejoy, C. and Johnson, S. (2009) 'A Longitudinal Study of Achievement Goals for College in General: Predicting Cumulative GPA and Diversity in Course Selection' in *Contemporary Educational Psychology*, 34, pp. 113–19.

Dweck, C. (2014) 'On Motivating Through Obstacle' available at http://www.youtube.com/watch?v=vw1pgbpVb9Q&feature=related (accessed December 2011).

Dweck, C. and Elliott, E. (1988) 'A Social-Cognitive Approach to Motivation and Personality' in *Psychological Review*, 95:2, pp. 256–73.

Flink, C., Boggiano, A. and Barrett, M. (1990) 'Controlling Teaching Strategies: Undermining Children's Self-determination and Performance' in *Journal of Personality and Social Psychology*, 59, pp. 916–24.

Grolnick, W. and Ryan, R. (1989) 'Parent Styles Associated with Children's Self-Regulation and Competence in School' in *Journal of Educational Psychology*, 81, pp. 143–54.

Huang, C. (2011) 'Discriminant and Criterion-Related Validity of Achievement Goals in Predicting Academic Achievement: A Meta-Analysis' in *Journal of Educational Psychology*, 104, pp. 48–73.

Livingstone, R. (1941) *The Future in Education*, Cambridge: Cambridge University Press, cited in G. Claxton (2007) 'Expanding Young People's Capacity to Learn' in *British Journal of Educational Studies*, June 2007, pp. 1–20.

Marsh, H. and Craven, R. (2006) 'Reciprocal Effects of Self-Concept and Performance from a Self-Esteem, Self-Concept, and Performance 20 Multidimensional Perspective: Beyond Seductive Pleasure and Unidimensional Perspectives' in *Perspectives on Psychological Science*, 1: 133–63.

Paulick, I., Watermann, R. and Nückles, M. (2013) 'Achievement Goals and School Achievement: The Transition to Different School Tracks in Secondary School' in *Contemporary Educational Psychology*, 38, pp. 75–86.

Ryan, R. and Connell, J. (1989) 'Perceived Locus of Causality and Internalization: Examining Reasons for Acting in Two Domains' in *Journal of Personality and Social Psychology*, 57, pp. 749–61.

Seaton, M., Parker, P., Marsh, H., Craven, R. and Seeshing Yeung, A. (2014) 'The Reciprocal Relations Between Self Concept, Motivation and Achievement: Juxtaposing Academic Self-Concept and Achievement Goal Orientations for Mathematics Success' in *Educational Psychology*, 2014, 34:1, pp. 49–72 at http://dx.doi.org/10.1080/01443410.2013.825232 (accessed January 2015).

4

Independent Mathematicians

One might think that the wish to develop independent thinkers and workers was a recent educational goal but here is a quote from 1961:

> If we value independence, if we are disturbed by the growing conformity of knowledge, of values, of attitudes, which our present system induces, then we may wish to set up conditions of learning which make for uniqueness, for self-direction, and for self-initiated learning.
>
> Rogers, p. 292

In 2008 the Quality Improvement Agency was urging the same approach: 'To give learners more responsibility for work or learning helps learners to make informed choices and take responsibility for deciding what they need to do in order to learn' (QIA, 2008: 1). And, Alexander (2010) in his extensive survey of primary education identifies independence as one of the twelve aims for primary education. He proposes 'autonomy' and within this he says, 'it enables the child to translate knowledge into meaning; it encourages that critical independence of thought which is essential both to the growth of knowledge and to citizenship' (p. 197). In reporting comments from adults he noted that 'some proposed that an important aim for education was developing children's 'autonomous thinking', 'the capacity to make reasoned choices', 'personal responsibility' and 'respect for themselves' (p. 185). It appears that independence is a wish from schools and from many parents but one has to question whether teachers and schools actually encourage independence or unwittingly create a dependency culture. Teachers, in a need for control, may suppress independence in favour of control? If we truly want children to be independent learners, what actions should we be taking? I would suggest that a typical mathematics lesson, more than many other subjects, is driven by a dependency culture due to the way it is taught as much as by the nature of the subject itself.

What do we mean by independence?

A truly independent person would be expected to make their own decisions, would be flexible when facing situations or working with others, would be able to take responsibility when carrying out tasks, would be well motivated, able to work on his or her own or within a group and be able to seek out information. 'According to Bandura's social cognitive theory, individuals are self-organizing, pro-active and self-regulating rather than reactive and shaped by external events' (cited in Pajares, 2002: 116). It may be that this is what we wish for and in reality children have varying degrees of independence. It is probable that independence also varies according to the situation a child finds themselves in. For example, a child can be an independent reader enjoying many story books but at the same time be very dependent on adult help when learning music or mathematics.

Independence or self-determination could be seen, like Deci et al. (1991), in their four stages starting with external regulation with the teacher exercising reward and punishment, moving to the child recognizing the rules and tending to conform as they are aware of the existence of the rewards and punishments. This would be followed by the child internalizing the rules and agreeing with them and therefore becoming more willing to go along with them. Finally the child reaches a point where he or she values the rules and sees them as an important part of the way he or she conducts his or her self. True independence would follow with actions being intrinsically motivated. Where on this continuum does your mathematics teaching lie and is it the same for all the children in the class? If not, would you consider treating some children differently?

This theory chimes with the work of Glaser (cited in Alexander, 2010: 416) who describes the move towards expertise in professional activities. Glaser identifies three cognitive stages: 'externally supported', 'transitional' and 'self-regulatory'. Alexander suggests this is the essence of teacher development, moving from dependency to autonomy – 'like exceptional performance in any sphere, [it] lies beyond mere competence and adds a higher degree of artistry, flexibility and originality'. I would argue that a similar model can be applied to children in their learning; ideally to move from dependency to autonomy.

I have been in schools where teachers have desired children to explore and investigate mathematics for themselves and found that the children seem not able to engage in this style of activity. Being asked to move instantly from a very structured, teacher-driven style of mathematics such as completing worksheets or pages of a text book has proved too difficult. The children do not have the skill set or experience of enquiry and are unable to engage in decision-making situations. The teacher may need to not only take the children through Deci's stages but also teach the skills of enquiry. This could be very worthwhile as they will be beneficial in many subjects other than mathematics.

When eighty primary school teachers were surveyed by Williams (2003) between them they gave fifteen reasons why children should be encouraged to be independent. They found the more independent children:

- had higher self-esteem
- had greater self-motivation
- were more confident
- were less attention seeking
- were able to resist peer pressure
- respected the view of others
- had the ability to take responsibility
- were good time managers
- had good self-discipline
- were more trustworthy
- were active learners
- gained satisfaction from personal success
- were able to communicate well
- were risk takers
- enjoyed challenge

Williams, p. 23

Teachers also found that the more independent children could work to a higher standard and were more socially adept (p. 24). This is an impressive list and for children to have these skills in mathematics would enable them to progress well.

Having identified the qualities enhanced by independence, how might the teacher increase the chances of this happening in the mathematics lesson? Again, we can turn to Williams' research to find ways of developing independent learning in children. She offers seventeen strategies for encouraging independent learning (pp. 92–3). Of these, several seem particularly pertinent to the mathematics lesson.

'Encouraging children to select and use a range of resources' and 'Providing tasks that benefit from a degree of independent work'

Are there opportunities for children to decide which resources they will need to complete a task or solve a problem or are they always provided? Are the resources readily available for selection or do the children need to ask permission to use each one? If the resources are available have they learned to take care of them and not be wasteful? Consider the two tasks given in the Measuring the playground box.

Measuring the playground

Task 1: Using the tape measure, measure the length of the playground in two places and the width in two places and then draw a plan on a scale of 1 cm to 2 m on 1 cm² paper.

Task 2: Draw a plan of the playground to scale.

In the first task the teacher has set out what the children will need and how to complete the task. In the second task the children have to decide what equipment they will need, where to measure, what scale to use and how to display the plan. The second task requires the children to make many decisions. It requires them to think about how to do the task and calls upon them to apply several problem-solving skills. Clearly the second task is harder but they are making independent decisions and choosing to select the mathematics to apply. Is it possible to turn simple tasks around by wording them so that more decision making is involved?

'Giving children clear objectives and allowing them to judge when they are ready to move on'

A common practice in English schools is to write the lesson objective on the board at the beginning of the lesson. It is assumed that if children know what they are meant to be learning they are more likely to learn it. This seems to be a fair assumption although I am not sure writing an objective on the board for four- to five-year-olds is useful nor copying the objective laboriously into an exercise book is a good use of learning time. Better to tell the children and then get on and experience lots of mathematics. Shirley Clarke (2001) refers to 'success criteria' as opposed to instructions or learning intention. Success criteria are either given by the teacher or decided in discussion with the class. They inform children they have completed that part of the task. It is helpful to know where you are heading in some

Success criteria

'Teachers need to separate the task instructions clearly from the learning intention and success criteria, or children can begin their work without knowing clearly the difference between what you want them to do and what you want them to learn.' (Clarke, 2001, p. 21)

Learning intention: To calculate the area of an irregular shape

Task instructions: Using 1 cm^2 paper, draw an irregular shape like a puddle.

Count the whole squares and those which are more than half.

Give the total in cm^2.

Success criteria: Know that counting the squares larger than half balances out those that are less than half so there is no need to count them or match them up.

Complete the count ignoring the squares less than half.

Know that this cannot be entirely accurate but is reasonable.

mathematics (not all) and children are reassured when they see they have met the criteria. They will also be more aware they have not yet reached the criteria and can identify that they need help.

It is also nice at times not to have stated outcomes. Not all mathematics should be a step-by-step journey. More opportunities to apply knowledge and explore situations should be available where children state their own outcomes. Some teachers occasionally turn the lesson around and ask the children at the end what they think the objective was.

'Valuing children's work achieved through independent action'

Often, when children get to make the decisions within a task, they take longer and do not always go the way the teacher intended. When being pressured to get through a very full curriculum, this can be understandably frustrating for the teacher. Using the oft quoted example of would you rather have thirty sunsets painted all the same or a range of individual interpretations one can more clearly see the benefits of allowing free expression. Think of the skills and thought brought to a unique piece of work compared with following what the teacher has already thought out. Allowing independent action is about opportunity for decision making and exploration, even if the end product is not quite what the teacher expected, the child may have learned much more on the way. Consider how much each of the teacher responses encourages independence in the Recording cube shapes box.

Recording cube shapes

Teacher response when shown a page with many wobbly cubes drawn on it:

Teacher 1: That's lovely. Put it over there with the finished work.

Teacher 2: Tell me about your drawing.

Teacher 3: I think you have recorded it exactly how it is . . . well done. How many cubes did you use? Are there other shapes you could make with the same number of cubes? Why not take some more cubes and find out?

Some schools in England have added a 'child initiated' time to their timetable. This is when children have the chance to select their own task and use resources from those available. There is an expectation that this will be purposeful and it is noticeable how many children choose to develop something they have just learned about in more formal situations. Piaget would probably recognize this as accommodation. Others would like to label it as play. Either way, it is about ownership and building memorable links to newly acquired learning.

'Encouraging a creative approach to problem solving'

Many of the mathematical problems children are asked to solve can be termed word problems which are calculations placed in a pseudo-real context. Many examples can be found in text books where to solve the problem a child is expected to use the mathematics practised just before on the page. For example on a page teaching long division, '250 children go swimming on Tuesdays, 35 children can travel at a time on the coach for a session at the swimming baths. How many sessions are there?' It is good to see mathematics in context and for children to identify what calculation is required but it is not creative. Williams is asking for something more here such as children setting their own problem or devising a way to solve a problem. If it is a real situation it is even better. Consider the Footprint and Monsters examples.

Footprint

The pot plant outside the classroom has gone missing. Can you find it and bring it back? First see if there are any clues.

(A large adult footprint is in the flowerbed. The children need to work out how to measure it and then eliminate the suspects.)

The key to creative problem solving is the opportunity for the child to take the problem in his or her chosen direction. A small amount of starting information, choosing the rules, challenging rules and asking further questions are often part of very satisfying problem solving.

Monsters

This activity was generated from a particularly difficult problem-solving page about aliens in the SPMG scheme. Instead of working through the page the children were asked to design their own alien monster and decide on a growth rate for it. E.g. an extra arm each year and a doubling in size. They were then asked to apply their rule for the first ten years. Then asked what their monster would look like after fifty years.

Finally, they were given the early growth rate of a real baby over the first six months and asked to comment on an extrapolation of the figures. (Growth slows down quite dramatically otherwise we would truly be giants!)

'Encouraging peer support'

Another aspect of working which can encourage independence is to carry out tasks in pairs or small groups. Strangely, mathematics is sometimes seen as a subject you always do on your own in silence. And yet, as adults, working together is often successful and pleasurable. Teachers have to weigh the balance between ensuring each child can demonstrate understanding and the benefits of peer learning. I once read about a teacher who introduced a mathematics 'help!' box into his classroom. Children wrote down the mathematics they were finding difficult and posted the slip of paper into the box. The teacher then addressed the difficulties in the following lesson. In the first few weeks there was a flood of papers and then strangely it began to tail off until there were hardly any. Apparently, once a child had articulated a difficulty, peer/peer discussion took place and many difficulties were being resolved before there was a need to write for help – the power of peer support in action.

'Providing models and frameworks to support investigation rather than only supplying the answers'

There have been several attempts to provide supporting headings or frames to help children solve problems or investigate. Most notable in mathematics are those offered by Burton in *Thinking Things Through* (1984), Askew in *Primary Mathematics* (2004) and Garrard in *I don't know, let's find out* (1986). There is little conclusive evidence to say any particular method always works as problems and investigations are often unique and one example will not necessarily help solve the next. However working together with children to show them how to untangle the words, select the calculations and check the reasonableness of the answer is always valuable. To articulate the 'how' will help.

'Allowing children to try things out and to make mistakes' and 'Allowing time to talk and for expression of views and concerns'

There is something demoralizing about seeing a page of red crosses in an exercise book. All those calculations and every one is wrong and every one has to be corrected. It seems such a waste of time. Would more talk before doing the work have helped? In one European country children are given one calculation to do for homework but they are expected to come to the lesson ready to discuss how they calculated the answer. This way 'views and concerns' are expressed and difficulties clarified. It does not necessarily take twenty practice calculations to ensure understanding. One opportunity to talk about the method either with a teacher or a fellow pupil could establish the correct procedure and a few examples to secure the method in a child's memory.

'Encouraging children to be involved in planning and assessing their own learning'

This is a big step along the independence spectrum and maybe only a few children can achieve this in a significant way but smaller choices will move children towards this decision-making approach. Maybe which order the child does three tasks; maybe how long a child thinks he will take to complete a piece of work; maybe choosing an either/or problem to solve; maybe reporting back on something they have done and how they could have improved it (a data collection for example). By asking children to judge whether they need more explanation or more practise on a mathematics topic or are ready to move on, you are encouraging self-assessment.

'Using clear questions and explanations so that children can adopt similar techniques'

Sometimes it is quite hard to articulate how a piece of mathematics works and once you have muddled children it is very hard to unmuddle them. Explanations need to be thought out and be clear and concise. In everyday life we may do some mathematics but as adults we are not asked to explain how it works. Explanations require a greater depth of understanding (Nola, 1997). It is a bit like being able to ride a bicycle and being able to take it apart and put it together again. Teachers have to do something similar when teaching mathematics. This requires a security of knowledge and is part of preparing lessons. Questioning is also an art. The teacher might have a series of questions ready to ask but the best ones are those which challenge the children and those which respond to the children's comments. It is too easy to get into the question-answer-approve routine and then move on without exploring the potential of what a child is offering.

'Introducing strategies for organizing finished and unfinished work'

How much time do teachers allow for discussing corrections and misconceptions? With the pressure of the curriculum causing hasty visits to topics sometimes children are sent away to do corrections without any new knowledge to help them or they do not have time to correct their understanding at all. It is so difficult to allow time if the teacher is expected to keep the whole class moving through work at the same time. Some will have grasped the concept and others will need more time. Does the teacher leave a topic and move on and hope the child will understand better on the next visit to the topic or does the teacher stay on a topic until there is sufficient understanding? Telling the time is a good example where there is a huge disparity of understanding. It is for the teacher to judge the right time to revisit and the right time to move on. Small group support can help those who are struggling. Good records of individual achievement can help the teacher plan the appropriate level of mathematics for each child.

It is crucial that children do understand a topic before moving on because mathematics is in many cases hierarchical. A lack of understanding at one level will escalate when a further, dependent level is taught. For example, not knowing about commutativity (3×4 has the same answer as 4×3) makes working out multiplications more challenging.

These are some of the ways in which teachers can encourage and develop children's independence in the classroom. If applied consistently across subjects children will start to manage their own learning. If children feel they have ownership of something they are more likely to engage in it and gain reward from it. Much more can be said about encouraging independent learning but hopefully this chapter has unwrapped what we might expect of children and prompted some ways of working in the mathematics lesson beyond a dependency culture which can so easily be assumed. I leave the last words to Margaret Donaldson:

> We must apply ourselves. We must become able to guide and direct our own minds. Thus the need for discipline appears. And though it is self-discipline that is in question, this is not easy to acquire unaided.
>
> Donaldson, 1992: 252–3

References

Alexander, R. (ed.) (2010) *Children, Their World, Their Education: Final Report and Recommendations of the Cambridge Primary Review*, Abingdon: Routledge.

Askew, M. (ed.) (2004) *Primary Mathematics*, Abingdon: Hodder and Stoughton.

Burton, L. (1984) *Thinking Things Through*, Oxford: Blackwell.

Clarke, S. (2001) *Unlocking Formative Assessment*, London: Hodder and Stoughton.

Deci, E., Vallerand, R., Pelletier, L. and Ryan, R. (1991) 'Motivation and Education: The Self-Determination Perspective' in *Educational Psychologist*, 26:3/4, pp. 325–46.

Donaldson, M. (1992) *Human Minds*, London: Penguin.

Garrard, W. (1986) *I don't know, let's find out*, Leicester: Mathematical Association.

Nola, R. (1997) 'Constructivism in Science and Science Education: A Philosophical Critique' in *Science and Education*, 6:1–2, pp. 55–83.

Pajares, F. (2002) 'Gender and Perceived Self-Efficacy in Self-Regulated Learning' in *Theory into Practice*, 41:2, pp. 116–25.

Quality Improvement Agency (QIA) (2008) 'Teaching and Learning Programme: Developing the Expert Teacher', available at http://tlp. excellencegateway.org.uk/tlp/xcurricula/el/documents/independence (accessed October 2011).

Rogers, C. (1961) *On Becoming a Person*, Oxford: Houghton Mifflin.

Williams, J. (2003) *Promoting Independent Learning in the Primary Classroom*, Buckingham: Open University Press.

Part II

The Development of the Primary Mathematics Curriculum

5

The Map of Mathematics

There is limited evidence as to the effectiveness of the way mathematics topics are presented to children, probably because there is such a variation in what children bring to the learning situation, but it is worth considering two principles about learning mathematics:

- Progression through mathematics
- Connections across mathematics

There is a danger of treating each topic in mathematics as a separate entity. This may have arisen from the widespread use of text books where, on turning the page, you are presented with a new topic. The National Numeracy Strategy (DfEE, 1999) was based on the premise that short visits to topics revisited several times a year was more effective. The danger is that the curriculum becomes very fragmented and children do not see the connections between topics. It is for the teacher to recognize the progression and connections between mathematics topics. Maybe it is useful to imagine mathematics as a 3D map. It grows upward in knowledge and skills, providing depth, but it also interconnects across the topics like an ordinary 2D map.

Progression through topics

Most curricula are strong on progression, dividing topics into bite-sized 'chunks' which, in the English primary school, are taught by a different teacher each year. The strength of designating particular chunks is that there is little chance of teaching the same mathematics year after year. It could be argued that this ensures progression and to some extent this is true. However, if we look at the mathematical make-up of a typical class we find children with a range of understanding and speed of learning. Inevitably, some children will struggle to learn the mathematics and others will grasp it quickly and be eager to move on. There is no easy solution to this problem. Various strategies have been tried such as setting, key objectives which must be learned, grouping, working as a whole class sharing the learning or recapping before moving on to a new topic.

Why is it a problem in mathematics which is not so evident in other subjects? Mathematics is often considered to be hierarchical, which in many cases it is, and that children need a sound knowledge of prior mathematics to move with confidence on to new topics. For example, division is challenging if knowledge of multiplication facts is weak. If children have to keep looking them up the focus on the concept of division is diluted.

Progression starts very early on with the roots of many topics being simple ideas which gradually get refined, measured more accurately or abstracted into formulae which can be applied in many situations. A good example of progression can be found in the topic of data handling. In considering underlying principles, it is interesting to track the early development of data handling and see how there are themes that recur and grow in complexity. Whether a five-year-old is working or an eleven-year-old the following skill-based functions are required:

- Questioning
- Observing properties
- Collecting
- Collating/sorting
- Counting
- Displaying
- Interpreting/explaining
- Extrapolating (Will it be the same next time? Does this tell us about other situations?)

Taking the aspect of display we can see a progression here based on the difficulty of producing the information diagrammatically but also the complexity of the data itself. There is no reason why older children should not use simple forms of display if they serve the purpose of displaying the data informatively. Simple data display methods include: set rings, Carroll diagrams and sorting trees. Block graphs can be as simple as children contributing cubes to favoured categories such as which flavour ice cream do you prefer? Bar graphs and line graphs have scales which can be challenging to devise and therefore appear later. For data which is continuous, such as forms of measure, line graphs can be used. Pie charts were drawn with a series of calculations based on degrees in a circle but now all computers have a selection of displays which can be used once the data is entered making display more accessible to younger children. Further up the school graphs will be used to compare two sets of data such as a height and arm span. These comparisons are usually plotted on scatter graphs.

Apart from scale calculation, often progression is governed by the difficulty of the questions asked. For example, an early question might be how did you travel to school? Whereas later in the primary school, the teacher might ask which is the best place in the supermarket to increase the sales of a product?

A lack of progression

If data handling is something that begins with observation and questions at five years of age and continues through to adulthood, an example of an aspect that appears to start abruptly part way through the primary curriculum is the topic of probability. Its roots do not seem to be recognized and many children have difficulty when they are asked to work out the probabilities of events occurring because they have no prior experience to bring to the situation and little understanding of the rules that govern probability outcomes. Children need to begin by noticing 'the same' and 'different'. They need to be able to 'observe', 'remember' and 'compare'. They need to have experience of prediction; the what might happen next questions. Language is important. Also relating the mathematics to children's experience is a useful approach to this concept. An example of this, rooted in the everyday, is sorting the washing line in Will it rain today?

Will it rain today?

A line is strung across the classroom which children can reach with pegs attached. Cards are handed out and children asked to place them on the line with 'certain' at one end and 'impossible' at the other. Once they have been placed, a discussion proceeds using vocabulary such as 'likely', 'unlikely' and 'even chance'. Cards might display some of the following comments:

- It will rain today.
- It will rain sometime in the next week.
- Manchester United will win the FA cup.
- Tossing a coin it will come down heads.
- I will see a UFO this month.
- If I turn over 49 cards an ace will appear at some point.
- Someone in the class has a birthday this week.
- The Head Teacher will hold an assembly this Friday.

The key ideas here are to develop a sense of likelihood and certainty. Discussion often touches upon the difficulty of absolute certainty when considering future events. The other key point is to distinguish between 'mathematical probability' and 'observed probability'. Mathematical probability is when you work out the odds of something happening. For example, the chances of a coin landing on a particular side is 1 in 2 as the choices are one side or the other. However if a coin is actually tossed 10 times it is unlikely there will be 5 heads and 5 tails. The result of doing the coin tossing is observed probability and is a form of data collection. (Actually, the more tosses you make the closer you get to the mathematical probability. What does 100 tosses produce?)

This is the simple end of the topic but it starts to give children the language of possible outcomes, the realization that you need to focus on one aspect and compare it to all the possibilities. A table showing all possible outcomes is often helpful. It is vital that children grasp these underlying principles to be able to progress in their understanding. Do we articulate principles when discussing mathematics with children?

Noting the experiences of children enables teachers to plot the progression through topics and choose a suitable starting point when revisiting a topic. This information might come from records kept by previous teachers or quick oral assessments made at the start of the topic. Continuity is the key to enable children to build up sound concepts.

Connections across mathematical topics

There is a limited amount of evidence that teachers who make connections with different parts of the mathematics curriculum are more effective than those who take a more didactic or a discovery approach (Askew et al., 1997). One of the drawbacks of making short visits to different mathematical topics or working from a text book which does a page or two of one topic and then moves on to the next is that children build the topics as separate concepts in their mind. To break down this isolating effect it has been suggested that it is good to make connections across topics. This may take the form of the teacher saying, 'Do you remember when …' and thus drawing attention to the links with other aspects of mathematics. It may be that the mathematics is presented to deliberately draw out the links. For example, how many children realize that 2^2 can be shown as an area of 2×2 or how it can be plotted on a graph. At a simple level the connection between arrays and multiplication tables can be demonstrated as cubes or pegs arranged in rectangles (a 2×2 square). Also 2×2 can be shown as 4 multilink cubes covering the base of a square box leading into images of area and then volume and cubic numbers as layers are added.

The use of these varied images can pull the mathematical map into focus as interrelated topics rather than a series of linear progressions. This should make understanding easier as well as giving children the opportunity to approach problems from different angles. By building many neural links this will make the mathematics more available and help children to become functional mathematicians rather than children who have isolated collections of mathematical facts.

The curriculum is the content – the maths to be taught

In England the days when each teacher taught what they wanted in mathematics are gone. In the past most teachers in primary school depended on the text book to guide them. These books were, and often still are, written by mathematics teachers. Some well known authors of the time were Harold Fletcher, Elizabeth Williams and Hilary Shuard and the Scottish Primary Mathematics Group (SPMG) who were a group of teachers.

Major influences on the teaching of mathematics in English primary schools were the Nuffield Project (1964–71) and the Plowden Report (CACE 1967) which urged schools to take a 'discovery' approach. Prime Minister Jim Callaghan's 'Great Debate' speech (1976) put Education on the political agenda. *Mathematics 5–11* issued by the Department for Education and Science (DES, 1979) was the first government recommended syllabus. This was followed by The Cockcroft Report, *Mathematics Counts* in 1982 which influenced the style of teaching, introducing the idea of a range of teacher approaches to mathematics: exposition, discussion, practical work, consolidation of fundamental skill, problem solving and investigational work (DES, 1982: para 243). Three years later further government recommendations were published in *Mathematics from 5–16* (DES, 1985). This was the beginning of sustained government guidance and legal requirements. 1987 brought a consultation document for a National Curriculum (DES, 1987) which became compulsory in 1989 (National Curriculum).

The introduction of international league tables (IEA, 1994) in which England performed poorly, aligned with a need for better economic performance, provided the justification for a top-down approach. However, despite the introduction of national assessment, by 1995 there was concern about low mathematical attainment in some regions of the country. As a result the Numeracy Project was established and run by Anita Straker between 1996 and 2000. Before the project's completion it was rolled out as the National Numeracy Strategy (DfEE, 1999) and introduced for all children between the ages of five and eleven. The National Numeracy Strategy became subsumed into the Primary Strategy and then abandoned in 2010. The National Curriculum, containing the legal requirements, was revised in 1995 (DfE, 1995) and 2000 to align it with the Numeracy Strategy and yet another version was issued in 2014 (DfE, 2014). All these government initiatives, particularly national testing, have kept the pressure on teachers and children to perform in mathematics.

International comparisons are interesting but must be interpreted with caution as different cultures have different attitudes to mathematics, different types of school are entered in the tests and the tests measure a fairly narrow, traditional form of mathematics whereas the English curriculum is much broader and has more emphasis on application such as practical mathematics and problem solving. This is not to excuse international results which are less than most people would desire in England, but it would be a shame to narrow the curriculum to pursue a test result rather than teach mathematics which is appropriate and useful for a future society. Maybe we just have to get better at teaching the subject and society better at valuing its worth so that expectations are raised all round.

Having sounded a word of caution, it is worth considering that there might be approaches which could be imported into one's own country. For example, the 'real maths' originating in the Freudenthal Institute in the Netherlands can offer children meaningful contexts in which to learn new mathematics. The English curriculum borrowed the empty number line system of calculating from the Netherlands in the hope that children would have a better understanding of calculation through a spatial image as opposed to a numerical rule. So you can see, we do import methods and curricula from other countries but they do not guarantee success and may need considerable adaptation.

There is considerable resistance from teachers to everyone in the country being taught in exactly the same way. There have been attempts to produce materials for each day of the year but teachers know that all children are not the same in the way they learn or the pace at which they learn. Also teachers are likely to teach better if they feel they have ownership of the material and methods to be used. I recall finding it difficult to teach some of the lessons set out in books. I seemed to need to assimilate and accommodate the ideas and methods before communicating the essence of the lesson to the children. There is no denying published material and model lessons can be useful, but they have to be adapted for the specific children you are teaching.

Contexts can be helpful and they can also be confusing. If a child is familiar with the context they are likely to see the relevance of the mathematics. If the context is unfamiliar then the mathematics can be obscured as the child deals with all the new images and their possible meaning. This is particularly true in examinations. It can be difficult for children to sort out the relevant mathematical information. There are children who realize they are entering the world of mathematics and they look for the numbers and actions whilst there are other children who take the situation at face value and apply their own experience of the world. Is this a conversation to be had with children . . . and how effective might it be anyway?

There are many variables to take into account when teaching mathematics. The stage each child is at in acquiring mathematical knowledge, the effectiveness of the teaching methods used, the motivation of the children, the connectedness of the topics, the legal requirements and pressure of others and what each child brings to the lesson. It is a challenging subject in which to be effective, but very rewarding when you get it right.

References

Askew, M., Brown, M., Rhodes, V., Wiliam, D. and Johnson, D. (1997) *Effective Teachers of Numeracy: Report of a Study Carried Out for the Teacher Training Agency*, London: King's College London.

Callaghan, J. (1976) 'A Rational Debate Based on the Facts'. Speech made at Ruskin College, Oxford, 18 October 1976, available at http://www.educationengland.org.uk/documents/speeches/1976ruskin.html (accessed September 2014).

Central Advisory Council for Education (CACE) (1967) *Children and Their Primary Schools* (The Plowden Report), London: HMSO.

Department for Education (DfE) (1995) *Mathematics in the National Curriculum*, London: HMSO.

Department for Education (DfE) (2014) *The National Curriculum for England*, available at https://www.gov.uk/government/collections/national-curriculum (accessed September 2014).

Department for Education and Employment (DfEE) (1999) *The National Numeracy Strategy Framework for Teaching Mathematics from Reception to Year 6*, London: DfEE.

Department of Education and Science (DES) (1979) *Mathematics 5–11: Handbook of Suggestions for Teachers*, London: HMSO.

Department of Education and Science (DES) (1982) *Mathematics Counts* (The Cockcroft Report), London: HMSO.

Department of Education and Science (DES) (1985) *Mathematics from 5–16: Curriculum Matters* (HMI Series), London: HMSO.

Department of Education and Science (DES) (1987) *The National Curriculum 5–16: A Consultation Document*, London: HMSO.

National Curriculum (1989, 1995 and 2000) A detailed history of the development of the National Curriculum is available at http://www.educationengland.org.uk/documents/pdfs/2009-CSFC-national-curriculum.pdf (accessed September 2014).

The International Association for the Evaluation of Educational Achievement (IEA) has run the Trends in International Mathematics and Science (TIMSS) international tests since 1994. The recent results can be accessed at http://www.educationcounts.govt.nz/topics/research/timss

6

Young Children Learning Mathematics

There is so much written about young children's learning that this chapter focuses on two aspects which influence the teaching and learning of mathematics; whether children are born with a natural ability to do mathematics, and, some features of early learning which support mathematical understanding. In 2007 the English government published curriculum guidance for children between the ages of birth and five. It based its content on four principles:

- every child is a competent learner from birth, who can be resilient, capable, confident and self-assured
- children learn to be strong and independent from a base of loving and secure relationships with parents and/or a key person
- the environment plays a key role in supporting and extending children's development and learning
- children develop and learn in different ways and at different rates and all areas of learning and development are equally important and inter-connected.

DfES, 2007e: 9

It would be difficult to disagree with these commendable thoughts. The following interpretation was more controversial but this was the first time in

England that specific guidance had been given to working with this age group. It seemed to push the boundaries of responsibility and expectation further down the educational journey. Children enter the education system with widely varied knowledge and maturity which makes a prescribed curriculum very challenging to teach, that is, if one should be teaching a set curriculum to three-year-olds. However, the general principles help as they can be applied to children with a wide range of knowledge and experience. As 'birth' has become 'official' educational territory, it is worth asking if children are born with an ability to do mathematics.

Do babies have an innate ability to understand mathematics?

There is an ongoing debate as to whether children are born with a degree of mathematical ability or whether it is acquired? One could say this is a branch of the well-known 'nature versus nurture' argument. Is mathematics an innate quality and are some children born more mathematically able than others? It is difficult to find evidence for either. Research on babies' abilities to recognize situations which involve early mathematical content indicate that there is some awareness very early on and it might even be innate. In the absence of babies' explanatory language research is often based on observation of eye movement as an indicator of 'noticing' change.

An interesting experiment showing an early awareness of numerical difference was carried out by Brannon and Starr (2013) working with forty-eight children aged six months. They showed the babies dots on two sets of screens. The first screens retained the same quantity of dots but changed their sized and position whilst the second screens switched the quantity of dots between two numbers. The babies focussed longer on the second screen suggesting they were aware that there was a quantity change. The same babies were tested again at age three years five months with two arrays of dots and asked which had more without counting. They also gave them an IQ test as well as asking them to identify the 'largest number word each child could concretely understand'. They concluded there was a match between the quantity recognition at six months and the performance at three years five months and therefore these 'quantity abilities' emerge early and well before entering any educational schooling.

As in the above research, observation of eye movement is seen as an indicator of brain activity. Vurpillot (1968) observed older children's eye movement when asked if two drawings of houses were the same. The image was complex enough to need the children to scan back and forth and compare paired parts. Vurpillot found that the older children scanned and compared whilst the younger children were more likely to say the houses were the same even if they were not. From this it might be concluded that the older children had a better strategy and also that the younger children were not too discriminating about the use of the word 'same'. It seems that strategy might play a significant part in matching patterns. It is possible that some children bring these strategies to situations whilst other children fail through lack of systematic strategy use. In support of these findings I have observed that several five-year-olds are happy to name 'almost' shapes. They classified shapes with three sides but rounded corners as triangles. They had as yet not developed the exactness expected of mathematical concepts.

The interesting research above does not prove that there are definitely innate mathematical abilities but it certainly suggests that mathematically favourable neurological brain structure and development does takes place in the early years (Blakemore and Frith, 2005) and this early development has a long-term effect.

Alongside this awareness of difference there is some indication that children have a preference for symmetry rather than asymmetry and a liking for ordering objects. Bird (1991) when working with four- and five-year-olds noticed that they chose to 'structure' many situations. Through her work with investigations with this age group she observed some children chose to 'arrange' the materials and information as part of solving the problem. The children had an opportunity to sort and categorize information and, without prompting, this is what they immediately did. Bird extended this idea to working with a mathematics situation as an adult where she is seeking a satisfactory and meaningful way of displaying her data. Eventually she finds a representation which shows reflective symmetry (pp. 102–8). She considers such responses as 'embryonic' mathematics. It certainly seems that this sorting procedure is one which many very young children possess and can use at a very early stage in school.

In considering children's early number skills Gelman and Gallistel (1986) propose that young children (three-year-olds) when presented with a small group of objects can and wish to count. They based their conclusions on work by Beckmann (1924), Gelman (1972) and Gelman and Tucker (1975).

They also recognize that a parallel process of subitizing (perceiving) can be taking place and that it is hard to tell which is coming first and which is securing the information for the child, counting or perceiving. The point they make is that counting is a higher order skill which is unlikely to be available to animals and that young children employ counting at a very early stage. This still leaves the question of effective usage of perceiving groups of numbers; either small groups such as the arrangements on a playing card or arrays of larger groups such as might be used in displaying multiplication tables. At this point of a child's development it seems there is the potential for using and developing two strategies, the cognitive, verbal counting rhyme and the visual, perceptual grouping. Pattern has its role in both of these but structures must soon be employed to deal with bigger numbers.

There is mounting evidence of very simple skills used by babies and young children which are fundamental to mathematics. It is difficult to say whether these are innate or learned very early on in a child's life but we can be sure that they are at the roots of mathematical learning. We also have indications from these early years researchers that children learn at different rates as there is variation in results. Whether that is due to innate ability or environmental opportunity is also difficult to tell.

Significant aspects of early mathematics learning

Much has been written about young children's learning, foremost of which are the EPPE reports (Effective Provision of Pre-School Education, 1997 onwards) which carried out research on 3,000 children in the UK from 141 settings. They concluded:

> [T]hat the quality and effectiveness of the pre-school remained significant predictors of attainment and social/behavioural outcomes right through primary school. Children gained most from attending high quality settings, employing trained teachers, but the influence of home continued to be stronger.
>
> EPPE, 2008, in Alexander, 2010: 163

This indicates the influence of an early and successful start to education whether in a home or school setting. But, how is this learning taking place? Traditionally, we can turn to the theories of Jean Piaget and Jerome Bruner to gain an initial insight into learning. Some of their theories remain alive today in the world of mathematics education as they link well to observed practice and appear to reflect more recent neurological findings.

It is generally recognized that when young children are learning they are assisted by practical work and representations of situations probably before attaching a more abstract or symbolic meaning to them. Both Piaget and Bruner (1986) have described this process as a series of stages. Piaget's theory links the stages to ages of development, an aspect which has come in for some severe criticism and major modification. Notwithstanding, the move from direct experience (Bruner's 'enactive' and Piaget's 'pre-operational' stage) through representation (Bruner's 'iconic' and Piaget's 'concrete operational') to a more abstract understanding (Bruner's 'symbolic' and Piaget's 'formal' stage) do reflect, to some extent, more modern theories of development. Learning is far 'messier' than progression across all fronts and as Bruner indicated it is perfectly possible to move back and forth through his stages when confronted with new situations. For example, an adult is asked how old his niece is? He resorts to counting on his fingers to work out the answer which is an iconic or concrete operational response.

It is important to consider the relationship between practical, representational and symbolic because in mathematics these are major elements right from the start. Mathematics is a symbolic language, even activities as simple as counting use symbols (numerals) which have specific meaning and need to be transferred to many situations; therefore they are symbolic representations of quantity which can appear in different guises. This is what children have to grasp beyond learning the names of the numerals. This is the abstraction.

If we ask children to look at eight toy cars and eight toy animals and then ask them what is different about them we would get many answers based on detailed observation. If we then ask them what is the same what answers would we get? Something about colours no doubt but it would be delightful to get the answer that there are the same number in each group. This is the answer from a child who has imposed a numerical system on a real situation. They have transferred and applied their mathematical knowledge. Analysing this simple situation illustrates how complex mathematics is from the start ... and how able children are as learners!

Added to these general theories are observations of situations where effective mathematical learning takes place. Gifford in her book *Teaching Mathematics 3–5* (2005) explores this extensively. Particularly interesting is her conclusion that, 'we need to provide opportunities for children to learn through observation, instruction and rehearsal' (p. 17). There are indications that imitation and construction or practical activities are also effective approaches. Children observe how adults or others do things which they then display in imitative play such as shopping in the play area. More directly, children copy counting strategies when working with an adult. Here the adult is in an instructional role and the child observing and imitating. The play situation, whilst involving imitation, can also be considered as an act of rehearsal or creation.

Play, in itself, is a major part of learning for children. Again there are renowned advocates of the importance of play in young children's learning (Griffiths, 1988; Moyles, 1989; Bruce, 2011). They explore the many aspects of play. Griffiths in her book *Maths Through Play* identifies many practical situations in which young children can experience mathematical ideas. Play can be entirely child initiated or, a situation where the adult sets up a situation or gives a task but the child takes it over or, a task where the adult offers some kind of intervention with the purpose of drawing out the underlying meaning.

How does play help children learn? Sometimes this is hard for the observer to see as it often does not appear to be contributing to the required curriculum. However, apart from a brilliant socializing event it can be a rehearsal/practice of new learning, a building of links to a child's prior experience or a safe way to explore a new environment. Any of these three are strengthening the neural links in a child's brain and establishing a stronger set of long-term memories which will probably be required later. It also meets a creative need in children; a need which is often squeezed out as a child progresses through a tightly prescribed school curriculum. Do we attribute enough time and respect to the power of play in contributing to learning?

The idea of adult support or intervention is a recognized part of early years' teaching. Beyond instruction, adults work with children when they are carrying out tasks. This 'steering' of a child's thinking has been recognized by Vygotsky (1978), Bruner (1986) and Wood (1991). Vygotsky described a situation where another person helps a child to perform at a higher level. He describes the probable limits of the child's performance as his or her zone of proximal development (ZPD) (Vygotsky, 1978: 86). Bruner and Wood continue this idea, describing the assistance of another as 'scaffolding'. This term is nicely illustrative of the idea of support as they go on to say that the scaffold is gradually withdrawn until the child is able to work independently with the concept. Individual and group support in class is variable, as is the gradual withdrawal of support. We are good on support but do we consciously encourage the move towards independence by having deliberate withdrawal strategies?

The home is where we see scaffolding most in action. Parents play an enormous role in teaching their children to eat, play, dress, wash and generally become social beings. In school in large classes this support can be more dilute. In the early years the 'informed supporter' is often an adult but in the later primary years it could be peers that can support learning in some situations. I do wonder if the power of peer support is underestimated and underused.

It is not possible to do justice to children's learning in the early years in one chapter. I have selected only a few of the theories and observations about young children's learning which relate to learning in general and can support mathematics in particular. I do feel that early years teaching approaches apply to effective learning throughout education and it is sad to see some of the approaches rejected as children travel through the school system. As Alexander points out in his report on primary education:

> Children need time to play, to reflect, to repeat and to talk to peers and adults.
> Alexander, 2010: 164

References

Alexander, R. (ed.) (2010) *Children, Their World, Their Education*, London: Routledge.

Beckmann, H. (1924) in *The Child's Understanding of Number*, R. Gelman and C. Gallistel (1986), Cambridge, MA: Harvard University Press.

Bird, M. (1991) *Mathematics for Young Children*, London: Routledge.

Blakemore, S. and Frith, U. (2005) *The Learning Brain*, Oxford: Blackwell Publishing.

Brannon, E. and Starr, A. (2013) 'Baby's Innate Number Sense Predicts Future Math Skill', available at http://today.duke.edu/2013/10/babymath (accessed November 2014).

Bruce, T. (2011) *Learning Through Play*, Abingdon: Hodder Education.

Bruner, J. (1986) *Actual Minds, Possible Worlds*, Cambridge, MA: Harvard University Press.

Department for Children, Schools and Families (DCSF) (EPPE) (2008) *Final Report from the Primary Phase: Pre-school, School and Family Influences on Children's Development during Key Stage 2 (Age 7–11)* available at https://www.gov.uk/government/uploads/system/uploads/attachment_data/file/222225/DCSF-RR061.pdf (accessed November 2014).

Department for Education and Skills (DfES) (2007e) *The Early Years Foundation Stage: Setting the standards for learning, development and care for children from birth to five*, Nottingham: DfES.

Gelman, R. (1972) in R. Gelman and C. Gallistel, *The Child's Understanding of Number* (1986), Cambridge, MA: Harvard University Press.

Gelman, R. and Gallistel, C. (1986) *The Child's Understanding of Number*, Cambridge, MA: Harvard University Press.

Gelman, R. and Tucker, M. (1975) in *The Child's Understanding of Number*, R. Gelman and C. Gallistel (1986), Cambridge, MA: Harvard University Press.

Gifford, S. (2005) *Teaching Mathematics 3–5*, Maidenhead: Open University Press.

Griffiths, R. (1988) *Maths Through Play: Easy Paths to Early Learning With Your Child*, London: Macdonald and Co.

Light, P., Sheldon, S. and Woodhead, M. (eds) (1991) *Learning to Think*, London: Routledge.

Moyles, J. (1989) *Just Playing? The Role and Status of Play in Early Childhood Education*, Maidenhead: Open University Press.

Vurpillot, E. (1968) 'The Development of Scanning Strategies and Their Relation to Visual Differentiation' in *Journal of Experimental Child Psychology*, 65, 622–50.

Vygotsky, L. (1978 translation) *Mind in Society: The Development of Higher Psychological Processes*, Cambridge MA: Harvard University Press.

Wood, D. (1991) 'Aspects of Teaching and Learning' in P. Light, S. Sheldon and M. Woodhead (eds) *Learning to Think* (1991), London: Routledge.

7

The Role of Mental Mathematics and Its Relationship to Calculation

Chapter Outline

I have chosen to consider mental mathematics before discussing calculations as in England and some other countries such as the Netherlands it has strongly influenced decisions on how to teach pencil and paper versions of the four rules (addition, subtraction, multiplication and division).

Ian Thompson, in his book *Issues in Teaching Numeracy in Primary Schools* (2003: 145–56), gives a useful summary of the role mental mathematics has had in the English Curriculum since 1920. He points out that mental arithmetic was considered of little value in schools until the 1940s when its usefulness in the workplace was recognized. But it was not until 1982 when Cockcroft published his report *Mathematics Counts* (DES, 1982) that it was seen as essential. Some mental mathematics was introduced in the National Curriculum (DES, 1989) but two events moved it to centre stage. Bierhoff (1996) noted the prominence European countries gave mental mathematics when he analysed other countries' text books. At the same time international league tables (IEA, 1994) were being established in which England did not do well. We see a response to these events in the

National Numeracy Project led by Anita Straker in 1996 which introduced significant mental mathematics strategies. These were carried forward into the National Numeracy Strategy (1999) which stated that 'mental calculation methods lie at the heart of numeracy' (DfEE, 1999: 51). The English primary mathematics curriculum currently holds a strong recommendation that a part of each lesson is devoted to mental mathematics.

There still exists the perception that mental mathematics is solely about learning facts and the part of the lesson devoted to mental mathematics is used to memorize and practise facts such as multiplication tables and number bonds. There was also the tradition in England of daily mental mathematics tests, often with no follow-up discussion of errors and methods. But mental mathematics is so much more than this. According to Thompson (2003: 147) in the Netherlands 'they use the phrases "working in the head" and "working with the head"' in which the first refers to the mathematics where children know or work out known facts such as $3 \times 5 = 15$ because I know it always is. Whilst 'working with the head' might work out 17 divided by 3 from the known fact of 2×5 is 10 and then add another 5 is 15, therefore $3 \times 5 = 15$, which leaves 2 more therefore 17 divided by 3 is 5 remainder 2.

Exactly what is it we expect children to be able to do when 'doing mental mathematics' and what should we be encouraging? Mental mathematics is about:

- the informal methods used in the 'real' world
- knowing mathematical facts
- knowing unwritten ways to calculate
- confidence to use what is familiar to you (but maybe not taught)
- knowing when to apply the appropriate mathematics
- flexible thinking.

Real world mental mathematics

An example of 'real' world mathematics is the calculation of Value Added Tax (VAT) when it was 17.5%. As this was charged on services many people found a mental way to calculate it:

10% of £2.20 is 22p, 5% is half of that = 11p and 2.5% is half of that = 5.5p, therefore 17.5% is 22p + 11p + 5.5p = 38.5p (rounded up to 39p)

This is a lovely example of halving as well as informal mental calculation; now fading as VAT is currently 20% which is a straight division by 5. Other examples could be collected from family members and neighbours.

Confidence, rehearsal and flexibility

Confidence is a key factor in using mental strategies. Confidence comes from success and encouragement. This stems from the teacher's comments and the situations he or she provides. Much depends on individual children's knowledge and ability to recall. From an understanding of how children learn it would be reasonable for a teacher to provide opportunities to rehearse the mathematics so that it is established in long-term memory and can be recalled.

But more than this, the children need to be able to recognize situations in which to apply the mathematics. Children sometimes think they are 'not allowed' to use a method which has not been taught and therefore sanctioned by the teacher. (This is particularly so when parents try to help with homework!)

Knowing the facts is about learning them and we see this in the introduction of new mathematics and rehearsal through practise. This practise can be split into repeat visits to the facts but also situations in which they can be applied. The real test of application comes when children are presented with a situation which requires the application of these facts out of the context of their learning. This is an aspect which could be used more frequently in school, not in tests but in discussion situations. Pressure of time is often blamed for lack of rehearsal at a date removed from the learning but it is worth considering visits to single problem situations in the talk section of a mathematics lesson.

What facts do we want the children to know? Often mathematics in primary school is seen as just these facts, an essential knowledge base, committed to memory. And certainly a knowledge base is essential. A knowledge of numbers and their value, a reasonable collection of addition and subtraction facts, four rules calculation methods, the multiplication tables committed to memory, a collection of simple formulae such as length × breadth = area in rectangles; length × breadth × height = volume in cuboids; perimeter is the length round the edge; percentage is 100th part of a whole or a collection; measure equivalents including speed = distance divided by time … and several more pieces of useful information. None of which are useful unless they can be applied in context. This application can be described as the process of recognizing the appropriate calculation to apply and gaining a sensible answer. This is a key component of mental mathematics as well as written mathematics. Some of these mental processes are described as formal and some as informal. The formal processes are those which are nearly always taught and are often pencil and paper methods pictured in the mind. I have met many students who visualize a blackboard with the formal written calculation

23

49+

in their mind's eye. This can provide a solution but a confident manipulator of number will see 49 as 1 away from 50 and therefore create 50 + 23 = 73 and then subtract the 1 that they added on for convenience arriving at 72. The confidence to manipulate number in this way is invaluable and should be one of the goals in teaching mental mathematics.

Knowing unwritten ways to calculate is a matter of experiencing them. Generally this is part of the teaching of mental strategies by the teacher but discussion with children in whole class sessions can generate alternative methods too. Some of the methods suggested by peers may be adopted by others, but not necessarily. Opportunities to have a go at a peer's informal method could help, and active participation may generate further discussion.

Short cuts or useful knowledge?

Examples of common mental calculation knowledge, sometimes termed 'short cuts':

- moving the numbers a column to the left when multiplying by 10
- moving the numbers two columns to the left when multiplying by 100
- adding 10 and subtracting 1 when asked to add nine
- knowing a number will divide by 5 if it ends in 0 or 5
- finding multiplication answers by doubling e.g. 4 × 15 found by doubling 15 to make 30 and doubling 30 to make 60
- knowing that 10 × 9 is 90, therefore 12 × 9 is 18 more and is therefore 108.

These ideas can be applied with different numbers. For example, how do you know a number will divide by 3? by 4? by 6? How many 20's are there in 180? They are not single facts to be learned but processes to be transferred to new situations. By understanding the process, children can expand their repertoire of functional knowledge.

Flexibility is about how children approach a new situation or a problem situation. Good mathematicians are prepared to try various approaches and are quick to abandon ones which appear not to be working (Dweck's mastery orientated children?). This requires a 'repertoire' of informal methods to draw upon but also a willingness to change the strategy. We have all seen children who repeatedly try to apply a calculation which is not going to lead to a solution. You have probably experienced this situation – I am particularly good at this dead-end approach when using the computer! Try something else, do not repeat the one that does not work. High attainers in mathematics rarely repeat failed strategies and are quick to switch to another strategy. This is as much a matter of attitude as it is of having a bank of knowledge. Do children see failure and further attempts as acceptable practice? Can teachers develop a flexible mind set in their children? I do not know the answer to this question but alongside teaching and encouraging a range of strategies, it is well worth trying.

Confidence, flexibility, knowledge of facts and knowledge of processes will make a significant contribution to children becoming numerate. Whether in their heads or written down it is hoped they will be able to use what is known to find the unknown.

Transition to written calculations

Calculating mentally can look very different from more formal written methods. In many ways they were seen as two separate skills, one approved of in schools and one you used out of school or did not declare. Thanks to some forward thinking in the 1980s to 1990s it was thought that these two approaches should be mutually supportive. This was particularly so in the Netherlands and England adopted some of their strategies. The National Numeracy Strategy (DfEE, 1999) offered new direction to introducing formal methods with transitional stages between mental and traditional methods. The Strategy introduced the idea of informal jottings for children up to the age of eight which allowed children to indicate their sequence of thinking. It was also felt that it was more logical to record calculations initially from left to right as opposed to vertically as this allowed for numbers to be considered as their complete value rather than as individual columns which often led to nonsensical answers.

Informal jottings

42 – 27 written formally as   42

                                         27 –

Could lead to   25   as the columns are seen separately and the smaller digit is subtracted from the larger digit.

If calculated horizontally a child might count on 27 to 30 is 3, 30 to 40 is 10, 40 to 42 is 2 therefore 3 + 10 + 2 is 15.

Or they might start at 42 and say 10 less is 32, 2 less 30 and 3 less is 27, 10 + 2 + 3 = 15.

If they are more confident with subtraction facts they might conflate the last two steps 32 to 27 is 5.

By breaking down the calculation into understandable steps the children can be sure they are getting the right answer and they can use the number facts that they know. Rather nice is the knowledge that any subtraction can be turned into an addition which children find easier.

The 'empty number line' was introduced based on work done by the Freudenthal Institute. It capitalizes on the multi-step approach. What is gained in understanding might at times be lost in errors creeping into the number of steps and children still have to remember the steps!

The empty number line

145 + 67

145----------+ 50----------195----------+ 10----------205----------+ 7----------212

Again, children can use steps where they are confident they know what is happening. As the children become more confident they can reduce the number of steps.

145----------+ 60----------205----------+ 7--------212

As you can see this is close to a formal calculation but interestingly there is a tendency to start with the tens rather than the units.

Calculations are broken down into simple more logical steps which we now call extended notation. Mental mathematics strategies are built on a child's known facts whereas written calculations are a drilled method dependent on routines (recipes) rather than understanding. Extended notation is another transition point to vertical formal methods. An example is division calculated as a series of multiplications. This is not mental mathematics; it is an illustration of what the multi-step approach builds up to.

Extended notation using known facts

$$36 \times 72$$
$$10 \times 70 = 700$$
$$30 \times 70 = \quad 3 \times 700 = 2100$$
$$6 \times \quad 70 = \quad 420$$
$$30 \times \quad 2 = \quad 60$$
$$6 \times \quad 2 = \underline{\quad 12}$$
$$2592$$

The values of the numbers are retained throughout. However, it is easy to get lost in the multi-steps but it helps that children know why they are doing each step. Otherwise it becomes just another routine to learn.

Mental mathematics is more than testing what children know. A facility with mental mathematics is a powerful tool for any child. By knowing various ways of approaching calculations, by having number facts at their fingertips but most of all being confident in their manipulation of number will provide primary children with a strong basis for entering the world of mathematics whether it is in their head or written down.

References

Bierhoff, H. (1996) *Laying the Foundations of Numeracy: A Comparison of Primary School Textbooks in Britain, Germany and Switzerland*, Discussion paper Number 90, London: National Institute of Economic and Social Research.

Department for Education and Employment (DfEE) (1999) *The Framework for Teaching Mathematics: Reception to Year 6 (Draft)*, London: DfEE.

Department of Education and Science (DES) (1982) *Mathematics Counts*, (Cockcroft Report), London: HMSO.

Department of Education and Science (DES) (1989) *National Curriculum for Mathematics*, London: HMSO.

Dweck, C. (2014) 'On Motivating Through Obstacle', available at http://www.youtube.com/watch?v=vw1pgbpVb9Q&feature=related (accessed December 2011).

International Association for the Evaluation of Educational Achievement (IEA) has run the Trends in International Mathematics and Science (TIMSS) international tests since 1994. The recent results can be accessed at http://www.educationcounts.govt.nz/topics/research/timss

Thompson, I. (ed.) (2003) *Issues in Teaching Numeracy in Primary Schools*, Buckingham: Open University Press.

8

Approaches to Numerical Calculation

There are many detailed works on methods of calculation. For example, Haylock and Coburn's *Mathematics Explained for Primary Teachers* (1995), Thompson's *Teaching and Learning Early Number* (1997), Hughes et al.'s *Numeracy and Beyond* (2000) and Anghileri's *Principles and Practice in Arithmetic Teaching* (2001) to name but a few. In this chapter and the next I will examine some of the issues that arise from taking particular teaching approaches but have not set out to give a systematic analysis of primary school calculations.

Early number

Going beyond what we have observed of babies noticing difference in small quantities, the first formal steps in mathematics will be learning the counting rhyme. Counting to 10 can be learned rather like a nursery rhyme or the alphabet. But what rapidly follows becomes much more difficult – using the rhyme or even just parts of it.

I can count to 10

'I can count to 10, 1, 2, 3, 4, 5, 6, 7, 8, 9, 10.'

'Well done. What number comes after 6?'

'1, 2, 3, 4, 5, 6, 7 . . . 7.'

'Well done. What number comes before 6?'

'1, 2, 3, 4, 5, 6 . . . I don't know.'

Similarly, starting in the middle and counting back from 10 to 1 takes more learning.

What follows learning the rhyme is the matching of the numerals to the oral names. 'Find me a six in this jumble of numbers', and then, matching names and numerals to quantities. The counting of objects needs the child to ascribe one name to one object starting at 1 and ending on the last number spoken as identifying the amount in the group. Lots can go wrong here, especially if the group is not in a line. Have any objects been counted twice? Is it possible to place the objects in a straight line? This will make the counting easier. For those who are struggling is it possible for them to pick up the objects and place them elsewhere as they count?

Having achieved successful counting children will be expected to move on to addition of objects. They could use a 'count all' strategy where the objects are pushed together and the counting rhyme applied or they might be able to apply a 'count on' strategy where the first group is a given number and they are expected to count on from the given number to include the second group.

Alongside early mental and oral mathematics children will start to record their calculations. This could initially be in pictures or mark making (Gifford, 2005). Pictures, for a long time, will be one-to-one representations. Mark making, or tallying, does represent one-to-one in a more concise way so might be adopted earlier by young children and does not require recognition of number symbols which in themselves are single representations of a quantity.

For a while pictures and numbers may be recorded side by side until children are secure in the meaning of the numeral. For most children they will move fairly quickly to numerals only and an addition sign (+). At this stage recording will be from left to right (although some cultures record from right to left). Normally the quantities will be given and the required answer will come at the end but look at the boxed examples, which are commonly found in infant schools (five- to seven-year-olds). Can you put them in order of difficulty for children?

Degrees of difficulty

The following are all basic calculations and yet children find some harder than others. Order these in degree of difficulty and then say how you could help children with the hardest.

$5 + \square = 11$ $\square + 6 = 11$ $5 + 6 = \square$

$11 - \square = 5$ $11 - 6 = \square$ $\square - 5 = 6$

The problem lies with the unknown starting point if the child is using a number line. Either they can use trial and error by picking a possible starting point or possibly use cubes and partition or combine them. The most sophisticated approach would be to understand that the numbers can be moved around. They form a triad; three belonging together whether it is addition or subtraction (e.g. $4 + 3 = 7, 3 + 4 = 7, 7 - 3 = 4$ and $7 - 4 = 3$). This is an interesting way to learn number facts rather than as a list progressing from 1 to 10. It shows the relationship between numbers and operations and gives children a flexibility as well as more number facts.

The horizontal recording from left to right follows the practice of reading so more recently it is felt that this should be sustained for longer. Also, as previously mentioned, children see the value of the whole number more easily than in a vertical calculation where there is a tendency to treat the columns of numerals as independent calculations.

Vertigo!

Some errors that children make when doing vertical calculations when they are not secure in the rules and number sense. Can you work out where they have gone wrong? What would you do to help them? (The exchange numbers have been omitted.)

45	57	42	603	500
29 +	36 +	19 −	508 +	498 −
614	83	37	11013	112

Two of these calculations have the same misconception. All come from forms of recording incorrect exchange. The last calculation would probably have been done mentally if the child had looked at the numbers before applying the exchange routine. If children realize this, they are beginning to show a sense of number.

Most errors in these traditional vertical methods come from not remembering the process correctly as well as errors in simple calculation. Whilst the traditional methods of these single- and two-digit calculations are efficient, which is helpful, the value of the numbers is temporarily lost resulting in answers which have little meaning. There have been much greater efforts recently (in England) to develop children's number sense and provide children with strategies which enable a more meaningful approach. Practising doubling, halving, adding and subtracting 10 and generally looking for easy ways or short cuts has been the curriculum emphasis. Not only does this tie in with oral and mental approaches, it can give children the confidence to manipulate numbers.

Meaningfulness drives an interim approach to more formal calculations. By breaking down the calculation into smaller steps which maintains the value of the numbers it is hoped that children will understand what is happening. This combined with a better facility for number should lead to less errors and a wider base from which to tackle new problems. This multi-step approach involves 'chunking' meaningful pieces of maths and then combining them. For example, 3×16 might be approached with the knowledge that 3×10 is 30 and 3×6 is 18 and then put the chunks back together to make 48. The calculation is working from what a child knows and is therefore confident with. The fact that these calculations are longer has earned them the name 'extended notation'.

Multiplication tables have always been a benchmark of children's progress in mathematics. As a teacher, more often than not, I was asked by parents whether their child knew their tables. Partly, I suspect, this was because they had helped them at home to learn them and partly it is an easy and familiar measure of progress. No one can disagree that knowing multiplication tables is a useful collection of number facts. Ideally we would wish children to be able to know any single multiplication out of context rather than chant from 1 each time. Some of them are really tricky; 9×8 is always a challenge as is 8×7.

Rather than 'chanting' the tables from the start it would help if they had meaning. This would enable children to build up connective pathways in their brain and consequently find them easier to recall. Lots of work with equal groups of objects is a good starting point. This is a form of equal addition. For example, 3 apples + 3 apples + 3 apples is 3 groups of 3 which can also be shown as 3×3. Look at the 'sausages' teaser.

Sausages on plates

$3 \times 4 = 12$ agreed?

Would that be 3 sausages on 4 plates or 4 sausages on 3 plates?

As soon as 3×4 is put into a context we can create different images, each of which gives a total of 12. Here we have the question of which are the objects and which is the function or action. Usually the number of objects comes first and the function follows with the relevant sign. Therefore, 3×4 is really 3 objects repeated 4 times, 3 ($\times 4$) = 12. Technically the first image is correct. Once you move into pure number either will give you an answer of 12.

A pure number context for multiplication tables is a grid:

×	1	2	3
1	1	2	3
2	2	4	6
3	3	6	9

The advantage of the grid is it works both ways and it can be used for division. Children do need to master the way co-ordinates work to be able to use it. Larger grids up to 10×10 can be found in many classes and teachers let children use them when they need to concentrate on solving the problem rather than their attention being waylaid by the number fact.

One more useful approach to learning multiplication and division facts is the triad method, suggested earlier for addition and subtraction. This can be a good five-minute filler:

3	
	12
	4

This offers multiplication facts out of context but also shows that $3 \times 4 = 12$, $4 \times 3 = 12$, $12 \div 3 = 4$ and $12 \div 4 = 3$; four facts in one go – what a bargain. The mathematical relationships are illustrated. When ready, further calculations can be added. For example:

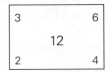

This leads nicely into factors at a later stage. The number 12 has lots of factors: 1, 12, 2, 6, 3 and 4; 12 is a multiple of all these factors. If this is a topic being studied, finding factor families is a nice enquiry. Which multiples belong in the same family (they have the same number of factors)? For example, 8 has 4 factors (8, 1, 4, 2) as does 15 (15, 1, 5, 3) so they belong in the same family. It could be fingers on calculators for this one?

Once children have mastered the single digit × single digit calculations they are required to move on to bigger numbers and pencil and paper calculations. The known facts, the chunking and the extended notation can be adopted with children refining their methods. Do children refine their methods or do they stay with what they first learned? Rather like starting at 1 every time they need a multiplication answer, the teacher will probably need to encourage them to move on. In England by the end of primary school (eleven-year-olds) children are expected to manage efficient pencil and paper methods of calculating. In reality they might still need to use extended methods. Reality poses another challenge; as an adult would you do a lengthy calculation or would you use a calculator? Which leads to the question, how much time should be spent teaching a method not likely to be used? Counter to that, it is firmly believed that children should be able to do a written calculation. It's just a question of which one.

Which do children find easiest?

87	$10 \times 87 =$ 870	$87 \times 36 = 3132$
36 ×	$30 \times 87 = 2610$	(calculator)
2610	$5 \times 87 =$ 435	
522	$1 \times 87 =$ 87	
3132	3132	

If they have learned the traditional method on the left, are consistent and remember where to place the zero then, next to the calculator it is probably the most efficient method. The 'chunking' in the middle calculation uses knowledge of tripling and halving which has probably been taught extensively before. However, the advantages of understanding, needs to be weighed against the likelihood of error in taking so many steps. In Italy the children are taught a grid method which has many steps but reduces every step to a single digit × single digit calculation. There is no easy way to describe what is happening as the numerical value of the digits is not obvious until the answer is revealed but the simplicity is in its favour. $23 \times 146 = 3358$ would be set out in this way:

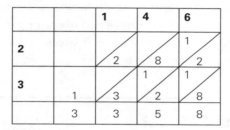

The same arguments apply to learning division methods. In division the added problem of the remainder on the calculator has to be dealt with. Do you want a decimal answer or a quantity answer as a remainder? Here, a way is shown of how to get back to a quantity remainder when using the calculator.

Which do you prefer?

Three ways to do the division of 3 digits by 2 digits:

```
    23 r 14      27 × 10 = 270        calculator: 635/27 = 23.518
27) 635          27 × 10 = 270 +      27 × 23 = 621
    54                     540         635 − 621 = 14
    95           27 × 2 =  54 +        23 r 14
    81                     594
    14           27 × 1 =  27 +
                           621
                 27 × 23 = 621
                 621 to 635 = 14 remaining
```

This is tradition versus chunking versus the electronic method – all require a degree of understanding and care. Some curricula require the first method to be learned. Which do adults use?

The numbers in-between

So far the chapter has been about whole numbers. At some point children need to learn about the 'numbers in-between' or 'parts of a whole'; decimal fractions and vulgar fractions. These parts of a whole are referred to as fractions and decimals and appear quite quickly in a child's life. A half is probably the most common, followed by a quarter. Decimals appear in measure and in money.

Rather than plunging into the notation of fractions it would be good to build up a strong idea of fractions through a range of practical experiences. In this way attention can be drawn to the importance of equal parts, the meaning of denominator and what the numerator represents. Also, for children to realize that a fraction can be part of one or part of a quantity; e.g. half of a bar of chocolate or half of a bag of sweets. Some examples of early practical activities are given in the box.

What is half of . . .?

. . . a piece of string?
. . . this pile of shells?
. . . the water in this bottle? (A challenge if the bottle is other than a cylinder.)
. . . the length of the room?
. . . the weight of this plasticene?
. . . the stones in this box?
. . . the letters in the alphabet?
. . . this picture of a puddle (A mirror is useful.)
. . . the flowers in the picture?

Beware of remainders when you are partitioning quantities.
Is it possible to find a quarter of some of these things?

By paralleling the practical with the symbols children will begin to build up a concept of these fractions and once secure they can build on this to establish new fractions and the relationship of fractions to division. After all fraction notation is also division notation; 1/2 (half) is the same as 1 to be divided by 2. This is true for all fractions although when referring to quantity it represents 1 group divided into 2 parts. This dual aspect can be a stumbling block for some children because it is hard to see that the same notation can have two meanings. It's that abstract thing again!

Decimals are probably easier (if only they didn't go on and on sometimes.) Early decimal experience is in money and measure but children do not always see the connection. The .24 in £3.24 is recognized as 24 pence and the .24 in 3.24 m is seen as cm. This of course is true but does not capture the general concept of decimals. It would be better to equate the decimals to fractions once tenths have been introduced. By keeping the numbers simple and familiar, children will be able to concentrate on the link between the two and realize that they both can represent parts of a whole or quantity. It is important to draw out the underlying generality by experiencing many contexts so that the knowledge can be transferred to new situations.

Exploring fractions and decimals

- If 1/2 is 1 ÷ 2 what happens when you divide 1 by 2 on the calculator?
- If 1/10 is 0.1, what is 4/10 in decimals?
- What comes between 3/5 and 1?
- Name a fraction between 2/5 and 3/5.
- If 7/9 is 0.7777 . . . can you guess what 8/11 might be? Check your answer with a calculator. Is there a pattern? Can you find more?
- What number exists between 1.2 and 1.3? Can you name two more?
- If 1/2 is 6, what is the whole?
- I spent 15 pence. This was a quarter of my money. How much did I start with?

These problems vary in difficulty and can be used at different levels. By changing the numbers they can be used on many occasions.

The trouble with decimals is that they do not always end so children need to learn about rounding up and recurring decimals. Take 6/11 for example; as a decimal it is 0.54545454 . . . forever. By putting a small dot above the 5 and the 4, the beginning and end of the repeating sequence, we can show that it goes on forever. Once children understand that the numbers following the decimal point grow smaller and smaller as you move to the right it is easier to cut them off in the rounding process. A tokenistic adding 1 to the neighbour if it is more than 5 deals with the tiny bits. A strong image of tenths, hundredths and thousandths is helpful in explaining this. For example, 2.26753 can be rounded to 2.27 to two decimal places. A little more challenging is 2.29653 as it becomes 2.30 or 2.3 because the 6 turns the 29 hundredths into 30 hundredths or 3 tenths.

In real life problems rounding up or rounding down is often required, usually based on what is reasonable in the situation. For example, rounding up to 1 would be appropriate when dealing with people but rounding down to the nearest six would be appropriate when dealing with packing boxes of eggs.

Percentages are another form of fractional numbers. 100% represents the whole and 1% represents 1 part of the 100. It is in common usage in the real world and an elementary knowledge is found on most primary school curricula. In most countries the monetary system is helpful as it is usually based on 1 unit and 100 parts, each frequently called cents or something similar. This structure offers a nice way in to dealing with percentages. Common questions refer to percentage parts, increases and reductions in costs or quantities. This requires finding the worth of 1% and then multiplying it up to the required percentage.

Through this brief visit to some of the arithmetic calculations taught in primary school I have hoped to show that children will grasp the principles more easily if they are working with meaningful situations, that if they are confident with the calculations they are using and the underlying principles are drawn out during the learning, the children will be able to transfer what they have learned to new situations.

References

Anghileri, J. (ed.) (2001) *Principles and Practice in Arithmetic Teaching*, Buckingham: Open University Press.

Gifford, S. (2005) *Teaching Mathematics 3–5*, Maidenhead: Open University Press.

Haylock, D. and Coburn, A. (1995) *Mathematics Explained for Primary Teachers*, London: Paul Chapman Publishing.

Hughes, M., Desforges, C. and Mitchell, C. with Carré, C. (2000) *Numeracy and Beyond*, Buckingham: Open University Press.

Thompson, I. (ed.) (1997) *Teaching and Learning Early Number*, Buckingham: Open University Press.

9

Mathematics in Context

Beyond calculation lies mathematics. That might be considered a controversial statement. Learning how to calculate is important but it is using the calculations to solve problems – that is 'mathematics'. And there are many opportunities to do mathematics in the primary school. There is measuring, working with shapes, timing events, solving problems, playing with mathematics and for children discovering mathematics which is new to them.

Contexts bring mathematics alive. Contexts bring meaning to many situations. For children, a context often helps them to visualize a problem. It can help them by prompting links to previous mathematics or life experiences. A context could be the way children enter the store of knowledge already in their brain. Is there a neural link to a past experience? On occasions contexts can confuse. Problems with lots of extraneous details can make it difficult for children to select the appropriate mathematics. Sometimes in the world of mathematics questions do not always behave in a common sense, real life manner. How often do you time how long it takes to empty a water tank or need to know how long it will take for two trains to pass each other? When did books and pens cost 2p? Do you really need 8 dozen eggs at 20p each? Meaningful, visually stimulating problems can be helpful as well as interesting.

A lot of primary school mathematics can be experienced in real or interesting situations. The following are some examples of mathematics topics which can be experienced in this way. Again, some of the underlying principles are discussed.

Measures

A significant amount of the primary mathematics curriculum is taken up with the learning of measures. This is probably one of the topics which is going to be used in adult life, particularly 'money'. Sometimes money is considered under 'number' but it can equally belong in measure as it is a measure of value and is nearly always used in context. Including money, there are six other forms of measure: length (distance), mass (weight), angle, volume, capacity and time, which competes closely with money for usage.

What do measures have in common? This was a question explored by Janet Ainley in her 1991 seminal article *Is there any mathematics in measurement?* In it she considers what principles underlay all types of measure. Considering these principles provides a good focus for teaching. Firstly, there is a need to understand the units being used and their relationship to one another. For example, there are 1,000 g in 1 kg or 123 cm is the same as 1.23 m. This extends further when moving into compound measures such as density, which is a combination of weight and volume, g per cm^3 or kg per m^3. Imperial measures still exist and the English primary curriculum expects children to be aware of the most common of these still in use such as pints, miles and pounds weight. It was fun to see the results when I set a piece of homework asking what units various things were measured in. Depending on who was helping, a mixture of imperial and metric answers came back. It generated a lively and meaningful discussion!

There is a need for children to be able to estimate. Will that box fit in that alcove? Will all this water fit in that bottle? Will all the boxes go in this crate? They will also need to approximate. This comes into scale reading whether it is on a ruler or a cookery weighing scale. Besides being able to use the instruments and read the scale accurately, including all those little marks in-between the numbers, they will need to decide which reading is the most appropriate. For example, is it sufficient to give one's body weight in kilograms alone or should one mention the grams as well? When building a cardboard model, should one measure to the nearest cm or the nearest mm? Measure is 'continuous' which means that there are an infinite number of readings between one whole number and the next so you can never be absolutely accurate, just near enough for what is needed and that depends on the context.

Progression is a major consideration for developing an understanding of measure. Generally children are taken through a sequence of descriptive language, comparison, arbitrary and non-standard measures to standard measures. These are then refined into smaller units or very large units and then combinations of units. However, some types of measure are more challenging than others and therefore are introduced at a later stage. Often this is due to the size of the numbers involved such as 1,000 g in 1 kg. Sometimes it is due to the complexity of the measure. For example, time has two scales (three if you count seconds) and these are based on 60 units (minutes) and 12 units (hours). Added to that is the unique properties of the analogue clock with its circular scale of half past, quarter past and quarter to. This measure only sits so early in the curriculum because of its common usage. I expect there are many teachers who fervently wish for the day we all go digital. Standard volume, on the other hand, is not such a common measure for children and tends to be introduced slightly later.

The table overleaf shows some of the main features of different forms of measure. Not all children will go through all the stages. Some children learn to tell the time and use a ruler at home and are ready to go straight into standard recognized units. However counting arbitrary time; one elephant, two elephants ... can be fun and worth combining with another activity such as making paper fly.

Money is another of those measures in common usage. It has a split personality – does it belong in measures or number? Interestingly those children who are mathematically confident tend to convert money calculations into number calculations and then convert the solution back into coins (Sangster and Catterall, 2002), whilst those less confident tend to work with the coins. The trouble with treating money as number is that not all the numbers are represented by coins so mistakes can occur when converting back to coins (children seeking the 3p coin!). It is useful to match the coins to a number line so that children can see what the options are. Lots of practical activity is also helpful. Again, those who shop with money at home will have a real advantage as they have plenty of experience to draw upon.

Table showing some of the main features of different forms of measure

	descriptive	comparative	arbitrary	non-standard	standard	sub-divisions/ larger	compound
Length	long/short, wide/ narrow	longer than, shorter than, wider than, narrower than	e.g. measure in shoes, twigs, shells	cubes, straws, rods, hand spans	m, cm	millimetres, decimetres, kilometres	speed (length: time), vector (length:angle)
Mass (Weight)	heavy/light	heavier than, lighter than, (using one object to weigh against)	stones, conkers, shells,	cubes	kg	grammes	density (volume:weight)
Volume	'big', 'small'	takes up more space than, less space than	conkers, toys, miscellaneous objects	cubes, anything the same	m³, cm³	mm³	density (volume:weight)
Capacity	full, empty		bottles, irregular boxes, teapot, cups		l	cc	
Angle	turn (dynamic) or corner (static)	left, right	quarter turn, half turn, full turn	right angle, degrees, acute, obtuse	90°	minutes, seconds	vector
Time	long, short	longer than, quicker than	comparing with an action, e.g. hopping 10 times	hourglass, yoghurt pot timer, one elephant, two elephants . . .	hr, min	Year, month, day, second	speed
Money	cost, pence	worth more than/ less than	tokens, exchange	tokens	£, p	€	value (£ per m)

Shopkeeper's change – counting on in coins

An example of 'real' world mathematics is shopkeepers' change, although with the advance of automatic tills even this is fast disappearing. It is actually counting on in chunks but the chunks are specific to the numbers available on the coins. For example, one pound (£1) is offered for goods worth 37 pence (p) when (100p = £1). The shopkeeper then says:

37p and 1p is 38p, and 2p is 40p, and 10p is 50p, and 50p is £1

This is very good for giving the correct change but if you were looking for how much change is required you would need to do a mental or written calculation; a subtraction or 'counting on'.

Data handling

Another mathematical topic which has opportunities for real experience and realistic contexts is data handling. It also has the advantage of being useful in other subjects. There are many ways of collecting and displaying data with their inherent degrees of difficulty. The ability to read data is very much part of adult life in the modern world so it is an important mathematical topic. Most computers can generate a variety of displays including pie charts. Devising scales from real data is notoriously difficult because usually it does not fall into neat numerical sections. First the range needs to be established and then a suitable interval chosen. Then it has to fit on the paper so a scale has to be decided and the axis set up before plotting the data. Alternatively enter the data into a computer. That is what an adult would do.

Often the beginning and end of the process are neglected. The process starts with a good question; what do you want to find out? Then, what data will you need to collect? How are you going to collect it? How are you going to display it? Finally, what is the data telling you? The interpretation can get neglected after the effort of doing the collecting and displaying. It is worth getting children to pose three questions for their peers when pinning up the graph for all to see.

If graphs like pie charts and time graphs are at the top of the skill list, the roots of data handling lie with noticing. Observing the properties of things will lead to establishing criteria and sorting. I observed one teacher holding up a pair of scissors and asking the children, 'What can you tell me about these?' She continued to ask the question after each answer, challenging the children to think further. Children are very good at observing and sorting. They notice the smallest details. The teacher's role is to ask questions about the sort once it is done. 'How many red cars are there?' 'How many green cars are there?' 'Where have you put the cars which do not have red or green on them?' 'Which colour has the most cars?' 'If you had another car, what colour might it be?' (extrapolation and prediction based on what exists). This type of questioning continues throughout the school. Maybe the children should begin to ask the questions.

All useful data collections start with a question because there is something you want to find out. In school sometimes this is for a purpose, sometimes just an opportunity to practise collecting data. The best questions arise in class from the children and the teacher sees the opportunity to practise or learn about data handling. The Real data questions box offers some questions which have been used by teachers.

Real data questions

How did you travel to school today? (This teacher used this on the day one five-year-old came by donkey.)

Take something from a story and have a vote with each child having a cube to register their vote. This makes a neat little 3D block graph.

What games would people like drawn on the playground?

What is your favourite flavoured ice lolly?

Do you prefer story books (fiction) or books about facts (non-fiction)?

Do you think children should do P.E. every day?

Is there a relationship between your height and your arm span? (Used with ten-year-olds.)

How did you spend the last 24 hours?

Is there a relationship between your height and the area of the sole of your foot?

How much exercise do you take?

Data handling lends itself to work in other subjects. It is ideal for cross-curricular activities. If you are a teacher who teaches across many subjects you are in the perfect position to use history, geography and science lessons to teach data handling in meaningful contexts. Adults always devise and use graphical data in real contexts; whether it is reading how your council tax is spent or managing a shop or running a financial service. All children will be meeting and using graphs in the future.

Ratio and proportion

Ratio and proportion are numerical topics but it is always useful to meet them in a practical context and best not at the same time, which unfortunately occurs in several textbooks.

Ratio is when a quantity is shared into two groups such as 3:2 which could represent 3 sweets for you and 2 sweets for me. There are five sweets altogether which can be ascertained by adding together the two numbers. But, 3:2 could also represent a total of 20 sweets in which case the 20 would be divided by the total (5) giving an answer of 4. Then 3 lots of 4 sweets would go to you and 2 lots of 4 sweets to me. The balance between the two lots remains the same; for every 3 sweets you get, I only get 2 which is another way of sharing the sweets in the correct ratio.

Ratios can involve more than two numbers. For example, a ratio of 3:2:1 would require an initial division by 6 or a 'doling out' method. A nice illustration of 'doling out' is when mixing paint or in cooking, either of which could be undertaken in class. Much later on in secondary school ratios can be expressed as decimals and people go on to use them for statistical comparisons.

Proportion can be a little more confusing and children need to be secure in the language they are using to grasp this concept. For example, there is a plate of 20 iced cakes on the table, 6 of which are iced green. We then ask what proportion of the cakes have green icing? The total number of cakes must be counted and then a fraction is created; green icing/total number of cakes (6/20 or 3/10). Proportion can be expressed as a percentage; 6 cakes have green icing, there are 20 cakes on the plate therefore 30% have green icing (6/20 × 5). Try the Proportion box examples.

Proportion

There are 25 children in the class, 15 are boys. What proportion are boys? What proportion are girls? Give your answer as a fraction and as a percentage.

12 girls form 20% of the swimming team. How many boys are there in the team?

At the end of year party 30% of the food was savoury, the rest was sweet. If there were 42 plates of sweet food, how many plates of savoury food were there?

This question is more realistic so you may need to round up or down as appropriate to the context:

The teacher ordered some bulbs for the school garden. There were 70 tulips and 120 daffodils. What proportion of the order were daffodils?

Practising routines and solving text book problems can be interesting but working with real situations and real data is exciting and if there is a purpose to the activity it is even more engaging. Contexts mostly help children to understand the mathematics so the more real activities the better as long as the focus of the lesson is kept on the mathematics to be learned and transferred.

References

Ainley, J. (1991) 'Is There Any Mathematics in Measurement?' in D. Pimm and E. Love (eds) *Teaching and Learning School Mathematics*, London: Hodder and Stoughton, pp. 69–76.

Pimm, D. and Love, E. (eds) (1991) *Teaching and Learning School Mathematics*, London: Hodder and Stoughton.

Sangster, M. and Catterall, R. (2002) 'The Mathematics of Money at Key Stage One (5–7-year-olds)' in *The Day Proceedings of BSRLM* 20:2 Loughborough, May 2002.

Part III

Four Key Issues in Learning Primary Mathematics

The Role of the Calculator

The use of calculators in primary school has been much maligned. Generally, those who wish to ban them cite evidence of secondary school children using them to do simple multiplication, producing ridiculous answers with no checking strategies and having developed few mental strategies. These are all good reasons to improve children's mental mathematics and checking strategies but these can be done alongside good calculator use. Most adults see calculators only as a short cut to calculation whereas they can be a very effective teaching tool.

It is interesting to read these comments from an Inner London Education Authority (ILEA) document in 1985:

> Vertical methods of performing the 'four rules' of arithmetic are rapidly becoming dated, just as about 400 years ago the use of the counting board in Europe was replaced by what were then new and more convenient pencil-and-paper methods of calculation.
>
> Ebbutt and Straker, 1988

and, from a government publication by Her Majesty's Inspectorate three years before this:

Mathematical content should take account of the potential of electronic calculators

3.16 The significance for mathematics of the fact that cheap electronic calculators enable the basic number operations to be performed instantly by the pressing of a few buttons has not yet been fully realised. For example, there is no longer any need for pupils to be held back if they are unable, in spite of long, frustrating attempts, to master these operations. Raw data, however complex, can now be handled so easily that mathematics can be given a greater sense of reality in what is done. The solution of a wider range of equations using numerical methods is now within the reach of many pupils. The emphasis in mathematics teaching can now be placed much more on conceptual structures and general strategies. A calculator will perform number operations accurately but will not give any help in deciding which operation to use in a particular situation: it is this latter task which is the more important and often the most difficult for pupils. Nevertheless, there is evidence to show that pupils' facility with number and their understanding of basic concepts improve significantly if calculators are used appropriately. Contrary to some popular opinion, *calculators do not constitute a threat to mathematics education. Used sensibly they will make pupils better at mathematics, not worse.*

HMI, 1985, pp. 33–4

It is worth quoting this passage in full as it puts the argument for the use of calculators in school but at the same time points out the need to teach the conceptual understanding of the mathematics being generated. Maybe this teaching was neglected in the rush for instant answers and as a result, in England, the traditional four rules pencil-and-paper calculation methods have more recently received a fresh boost through the latest National Curriculum (DfE, 2014) alongside a political belief in their essentiality. At the same time calculator use remains suppressed:

Information and communication technology (ICT)

Calculators should not be used as a substitute for good written and mental arithmetic. They should therefore only be introduced near the end of key stage 2 to support pupils' conceptual understanding and exploration of more complex number problems, if written and mental arithmetic are secure. In both primary and secondary schools, teachers should use their judgement about when ICT tools should be used.

DfE, 2014, Introductory page

So, maybe we have to wait a few more years before electronic aids will become the norm. It is fair to say, that in the interim, the various National Curricula for primary schools in England have adopted a more meaningful build up to these traditional methods and have significantly and successfully strengthened children's abilities in mental mathematics.

After the amazing results of the Calculator Awareness Number (CAN) pilot studies (Shuard et al., 1991; Duffin, 1996) within the Primary Initiatives in Mathematics Education research project (PrIME 1985–90)[1] it is a shame that calculators do not have a better image. It appears that part of the problem lies with adult usage of short-cut calculations being the perceived purpose rather than as a teaching tool in exploring the nature of number and its properties. A few examples might aid illustration of this point.

There are some areas of mathematics which can be enhanced by using the calculator to explore possibilities. Number generation, place value, computation, number patterns, decimals and negative numbers are topics which lend themselves to work with the calculator in the primary school.

The calculator can be easily used to generate numbers. Young children like to create 'big' numbers and to name them. Whilst there is a need to know about the various properties of number, the big numbers are exciting and gradually children will develop an understanding of their value. I recall a five-year-old child asking me the name of a number on her calculator. I named the number. She then said, 'How big is that?' I replied, 'Very big' to which she responded, 'As big as a field of flowers?' Isn't that the kind of conversation that starts a child on her mathematical journey? It probably would not have happened if the child had not had the opportunity to use the calculator. Simple number games help familiarity. For example, the following boxed activities help establish number recognition on both written and calculator numerals.

Name that number

You need 2 players, 1 calculator and 11 cards numbered 0–10.

Shuffle the cards and place them face down.

Player 1 takes the top card and asks player 2 to make the number on the calculator.

Both players check and if correct player 2 gets to keep the card.

(A number line is helpful if either player is uncertain.)

Harder versions can be played using different sets of cards.

---

[1] PrIME was a major, government funded project run by Hilary Shuard of Homerton College, Cambridge between 1985 and 1990. It involved selected schools in a range of local authorities with innovative work on focussed aspects of mathematics education. Calculators, working with parents, investigations were three of the topics. The CAN project was the most controversial but also had significantly positive results.

Heaps of cubes

You need 2 players, 1 calculator and 20 cubes.

Player 1 sets the calculator at a number below 20.

Player 2 has to make a pile of cubes with exactly that number.

They check together. (It is helpful to have a 0–20 number line available.)

A harder version is to ask player 1 to say how many more cubes would make 20. This could be checked together on the calculator

(This activity offers number recognition, counting to 20 and could involve counting on.)

Big numbers can be systematically or randomly generated but also patterns can be created by using the addition button. Repeatedly adding the same number starting from zero gives the answers to multiplication tables and an immediate introduction to the concept of multiplication as a form of repeated addition. It does not, however, show how many additions have taken place unless this is noted. This could lead comfortably into the use of the multiplication button as a short cut. It is important that children know multiplication facts without resorting to using the calculator but this initial work and opportunities to revisit the activities will help to develop an understanding of the meaning of multiplication tables.

Number patterns can be generated using the constant function. Try some of these from the Number patterns box.

Number patterns

To set up a constant function on most calculators key in the amount you want to add then press + twice. Then key in the number you want to start from and keep pressing = to generate the next number. E.g. to generate even numbers press 2 + + 0 = = = =, odd numbers 2 + + 1 = = = etc. A pencil-and-paper recording of the numbers is recommended.

Try:

- counting in 5s
- counting in 10s

- counting in 100s
- counting in 3s starting at 2
- subtracting 2s from 49 (2 – – 49 = =)
- subtracting 10s from 95.

What happens if you use the × button instead of +?

Number recognition is essential but it is equally important that children come to understand the value of the numbers and the pattern of the base 10 system that we use for nearly all numerical transactions. This involves an understanding of place value. Number lines, base 10 apparatus and 100 number grids are important resources that show this pattern visually and spatially. The calculator can support the worth of a number by offering quick and repeated experience of moving the numerals from column to column by multiplication and division by 10, 100 and 1,000. For example, what happens to 3 when it is multiplied by 10? and by 100? On the calculator many examples can be explored in rapid succession and a consistent pattern will appear leading the way to a generalization (What always happens?). The Steal box provides a game based on the happy families card game which can be played by two children and used to support an understanding of the value of a digit in its position within a number.

Steal

You need two players with a calculator each.

Both players put in a thousands hundreds tens and units number in their own calculator, taking care that the other player can not see it. E.g. Player 2 entered 2678.

Player 1: Have you got a 6?

Player 2: Yes (If 'No' the turn moves on to Player 2.)

Player 1: What's it worth?

Player 2: 600

Player 1 then steals 600 by adding it to their number whilst player 2 subtracts it from their number.

Player 2 now takes a turn to ask Player 1.

The winner is the player who removes all the other player's number. Occasionally a stalemate arises when it is best to start again.

The most obvious use of the calculator is for doing operations/calculations. The ultimate goal of learning pencil-and-paper calculations is to do them 'efficiently' and 'correctly'. Using a calculator offers an even more efficient method but is often challenged on correctness. With suitable checking strategies in place, such as repeating the calculation, approximating the answer or reversing the calculation, the calculator tops the speed list. It is understandable that society wishes to maintain pencil-and-paper approaches as education is a fairly traditional activity! Children need to be able to do mental calculation, calculator and pencil-and-paper calculations but above all they need to understand what they are doing. It is good to find a way to use all three methods to support each other in a learning environment.

The Stepping stones and Find the factors boxes suggest some examples that use the calculator to support and confirm mental calculation. The first activity sets calculator against mental arithmetic, the second is an opportunity to explore factors and practise multiplication table knowledge and its relationship to division.

Stepping stones

You need some large cards which a child can stand on with functions such as +2, +5, −1, +2, +3, −5, −6. (These are the stepping stones) and a calculator between two.

One child stands on the bank which is 0 and steps onto the first stone.

The rest of the children have to give the answer (+2 on white boards) and then check it on the calculator.

Leaving the answer on the calculator the child steps on to the next stone and the process is repeated. (Do not clear the calculator.)

Find the factors

16 is the answer to 4 × 4 but it is also the answer to 8 × 2 and to 16 × 1.

1, 2, 4, 8 and 16 are all factors of 16.

What are all the factors of the following numbers:

12   24   30   35   50   96

(The easiest way to calculate these is to do the inverse/divide. Give time to see if the children work this out and if not, pause for a class discussion.)

What is special about the factors of 4, 36 and 64?

As an extension the class could work together to find numbers below 100 which have the same number of factors.

Patterns and relationships are at the heart of mathematics. The calculator is ideal for generating patterns but observation of children doing these activities brings a strong warning. In their enthusiasm they can generate a number and then another and the first number is lost, the children repeat a function but give no thought to the sequence or why it is happening. This can be avoided by building in recording and reflection on the activity. Ruthven (2003: 204) has two helpful phrases to overcome this rush for results; *'diagnose – explain – reinforce'* and *'observe – predict – surpass'*; good advice for many mathematical situations. The Jumping down and Constant capacity activities provide examples where informal recording is required.

Jumping down

You need a calculator.

Start with 27 and subtract 3, subtract 3 again, and again . . . Record your answers as you go. What do you notice about the pattern you have made?

What if you start at 28 instead?

Try starting with other numbers and a different subtractor. Remember to record your answers and think about the pattern.

Constant capacity

It is good to start this practically in which case you will need 1 cm^2 paper, scissors and sticky tape.

Construct a box which will hold 72 cm³. What is its length, breadth and depth?

Using the calculator can you work out the length, breadth and depth of other boxes which would hold 72 cm³ exactly?

It could be that the calculator is where a child meets a negative number for the first time. If the number line has been used in class it is a good idea to extend it below zero. This, combined with the familiar strategy of counting up and down the line for addition and subtraction should establish a strong context for negative numbers. Real world examples of negative numbers are rare. Debt and depth below sea level are two examples. Negative numbers belong much more in the 'world of mathematics' and can be really helpful in supporting some of the principles of mathematics. The following boxes provide examples.

I owe you

Create simple money stories such as:

John went shopping with his Dad. He had £1 pocket money with him. He wanted to buy a comic for 40p and a pen for 65p. How much did his Dad agree to lend him?

Thanks Dad, I owe you . . . p. I'll pay you back next week.

What's the difference?

You need a calculator.

Start with 9 and take away 5. Now start with 5 and take away 9.

What has happened?

Does this happen with all pairs of numbers? Using a number line can you explain this?

Decimals appear at an early stage when using a calculator. They usually arise when a division calculation is carried out. This is fine if the divisor goes exactly into the number to be divided or an answer gives a recognizable decimal such as .5 or .25 but quite often a string of numbers is generated such as when 10 is divided by 3. Then the number of decimal places required and rules of rounding off need to be introduced. Interesting conversations can be had about appropriate answers in terms of size and reality. The oft quoted problem of the number of 40-seater buses required to transport a group of 769 people is a good illustration of a need for a sensible answer when children claim that 19.225 buses are needed or even 19 buses which leaves 9 people behind!

Decimal digits

You need a calculator, pencil and paper.

Choose 6 thousands hundreds tens and units number and divide them by 9.

Record your answers. Is there a pattern here in the decimal part of your answer?

What happens when you divide any number by 11?

Try dividing by other single digit numbers. What do you notice about the decimals? (If you extend the repeats in the decimal, patterns will emerge beyond the 8 digits on show.)

Making pies

You need a calculator, paper and pencil.

Draw three right-angle triangles and carefully measure the three sides of each.

Using the calculator multiply each side by itself (square it).

Compare your answers for each triangle. Is there a pattern?

Does it work for all triangles?

Questions often arising from calculator use

Here are some of the common questions asked by parents, teachers and the media about children using calculators. I have offered possible answers (adapted from Sangster, 1990) but you will probably have examples of more convincing evidence from your own practice.

Q. How should I respond when there is a pressure to show pencil-and-paper calculations?

A. Children learn in many situations where recording is not required, e.g. Physical Education lessons. When using calculators, forms of recording are often useful but they tend not to be in traditional form, however, they are still pencil-and-paper calculations.

Q. What do you do when a decimal number appears on the display before you have taught it?

A. At an early stage you might give the response that the whole numbers are on the left of the dot (point) and those on the right are 'a little bit more'. At some stage they will be ready to look more closely at that little bit more, for example, when you divide 3 by 2 the display shows 1.5 but the children already know the answer is 1½ so .5 is the same as half. (Try 1 divided by 2 and 5 divided by 2 to check.) This leads into common fraction/decimal equivalents and on to the value of numerals in the decimal places.

Q. Does the use of the calculator inhibit children's mental development?

A. It is very important that children have a range of mental strategies. The CAN research project found that children who worked extensively with calculators developed strong mental strategies because they engaged more with exploring the mathematics and came to 'know' the key information that we label 'mathematical facts'.

Q. Do children rely too much on calculators?

A. We live in a world of changing technology. Consider when your children will be leaving school; what will the workplace demand of them then? To use a calculator you have to know what calculation you want to do and how to enter that calculation. You have to know if you have a reasonable answer and it helps to know how to check that the answer is correct. Children with good calculator skills can do all of these things. Whilst the calculator calculates children are free to think about the mathematical situation they are tackling.

One of the biggest joys of using the calculator is the ease with which mistakes can be wiped out. No one minds starting again when it can be done that quickly. For young children the mind works far more quickly than the pencil. Calculators are good motivation tools, numbers can become fun and children's confidence in number manipulation can grow. Mathematically, their use can improve their level of understanding of number patterns, calculations, multiplication tables, large numbers, decimals and negative numbers, as long as they are taught to use them appropriately. The biggest bonus, for me, is that they can be used to explore numbers and calculations and to allow children to focus on thinking about problems without getting diverted by the effort of recording a long pencil-and-paper calculation. Calculator use in primary schools should be seen not merely as a computational aid but as a pedagogical tool which will enable children to explore mathematical concepts.

References

Department for Education (DfE) (July 2014) *Statutory Guidance: National Curriculum in England: Mathematics Programmes of Study*, available at https://www.gov.uk/government/publications/national-curriculum-in-england-mathematics-programmes-of-study/national-curriculum-in-england-mathematics-programmes-of-study

Duffin, J. (1996) *Calculators in the Classroom: The Reports of the Calculator Awareness Number Components of the PrIME Project and CAN Continuation Project,* Liverpool: Manutius Press.

Ebbutt, S. and Straker, A. (1988) *Mathematics in ILEA Primary Schools Part 1: Children and Mathematics*, London: Collins Educational.

HMI (1985) *Mathematics 5–16, HMI Series: Curriculum Matters No. 3*, London: HMSO available at http://www.educationengland.org.uk/documents/hmi-curricmatters/maths.html

Ruthven, K. (2003) 'The Pedagogy of the Calculator' in I. Thompson (ed.), *Issues in Teaching Numeracy in Primary Schools*, Buckingham: Open University Press.

Sangster, M. (1990) *Using Calculators in the First School*, Epsom: Surrey Mathematics.

Shuard, H., Walsh, A., Goodwin, J. and Worcester, V. (1991) *Calculators, Children and Mathematics*, London: Simon and Schuster.

Children Solving Mathematical Problems

Solving problems, the application of mathematics is the ultimate purpose of mathematics. Taking language learning as a parallel, mathematical problem solving is the chance to use the spellings you have been arduously learning to write a story or a letter. Real problems from the real world have limited availability in the school mathematics lesson but we create 'maths world' problems where the price of food is ridiculously cheap, all rooms are square, percentages come in multiples of 10 and all the circle calculations come out exactly, no rounding required! Mathematical problems appear in books to practise application of learned routines and they are usually included in exams. They can be fun and motivating too. They will be present in adult life and for some they will be required in specialized ways for work.

Mathematical problem solving is seen as difficult and often it is. Jones (2003) defines a problem as an activity where the route to its solution is not immediately obvious. Even more difficult is how to teach it successfully. Why? Because each problem is different and each needs the right key (knowledge) to unlock it. I guess there are as many problems in this world as there are keys. However, if we look at the roots of problem solving it starts off possibly earlier than calculation methods. As soon as children start learning mathematics the teacher uses words and contexts. For example, he or she might say, 'What is five take away two?' Then he or she might say, 'If I have five apples and I eat two apples, how many are left?'

This is not seen as 'difficult'. Children hear a fluent and simple question and then are presented with the same calculation in a familiar context. The accessibility is aided by having the problem spoken and then illustrated. As children progress through the curriculum the problems become written and sometimes utilize contexts which are alien to them.

Simple word problems – calculations with words

Carpenter et al. (1982) carried out a longitudinal study between 1978 and 1981 with 150 first grade children (six-year-olds). They researched types of word problem in addition and subtraction. The word problems were simple situations such as; Peter had 8 marbles, played a game and lost 4 marbles. How many has he got now? Their results showed that it was not simple! They identified seventeen different types of word problem which they classified into six main types (Carpenter et al., pp. 12–13):

- Joining
- Separating
- Part-part whole
- Comparison
- Equalizing – add on
- Equalizing – take away

Can you identify some of these main types according to Carpenter et al. in the Which is which –word problems box?

Which is which – word problems

Connie has some marbles. She won 8 more marbles. Now she has 13 marbles. How many marbles did she have to start with?

There are 7 cups and 11 saucers on the table. How many saucers should I put away to have the same number of cups as saucers?

There are 6 boys and 8 girls on the soccer team. How many more girls than boys are there on the team?

Fred had 11 pieces of candy. He gave 7 pieces to Linda. How many pieces of candy did Fred have left?

(Answers can be found at end of this chapter)

There are many other studies which make a close examination of similar early arithmetic; Ginsberg (1977), Gelman and Gallistel (1978), Greeno et al. (1984), Kamii (1985), Askew (2004), to name but a few of the pioneers in this area. The work of Carpenter et al. is used here to illustrate how the complexities of language make supposedly simple arithmetic situations more difficult.

Why is problem solving generally so difficult?

One might say the problem is each problem is different. Often there are many steps to take before the solution is arrived at. As soon as a problem is written down, a facility with reading is required. A child may be able to read the words but they also need to draw meaning from them. Unless they can understand what is being asked for they cannot get started. It is rather like placing a gate in front of the calculation. A gate which has to be opened before you can get to the action. It might even feel like several gates from which the solver has to choose! A mastery of language is required which is not always in line with a child's ability to calculate.

This could be helped or hindered by the context. A familiar context means that a child can bring experience to the situation to make sense of it. For example, 3 children are required to share 9 sweets between them. Happily the solution is easy, 3 sweets each. What if they had to share 10 sweets? In the real world they would share the tenth sweet between them or, the dominant child would claim the final sweet, or they would give it to someone else. There would be no question of one remaining in the bag! (This was a small but diverting problem which challenged some boys in my class.) One of the early national mathematics tests for seven-year-olds in England and Wales had many questions set in the context of a fairground. Very few of the children in my class had even seen a coconut shy. The context became an added hurdle rather than a help. Children's life experiences are so varied that it is hard to know when contexts can be helpful.

The next stage of the problem solving is to draw out the mathematics into a numerical calculation. This requires a good understanding of the question and knowledge of the mathematics. The mathematical knowledge has to be matched to the situation. This is probably the most difficult part of the process. Something has to link in the brain between the current situation and past experience. Luck is on the child's side if they have experienced a situation very close to the new problem. A broad range of similar past experiences is helpful. Some children are taught to look for 'trigger words'. These are words which indicate the calculation such as 'more', 'less', 'percentage', 'altogether', 'take away' and 'each'. These are useful clues but they can be interpreted incorrectly. For example, 'more' could be an addition or multiplication calculation; percentage could indicate a reduction or an increase. The meaning still needs to be interpreted.

De-contextualizing the problem to create a calculation is something that more able children do when working with money. They have realized that coin values can be turned into numbers, calculated and then turned back into money. Here we see an early transfer of knowledge to aid a different context. Re-contextualizing the calculation is another stage in the process where some children fall down. Having finished the calculation they stop. They fail to return to the original question to check what is required. The famous example of providing 7½ coaches for the swimming trip illustrates the point nicely.

Many school texts introduce children to a type of calculation, offer a series of practice examples and then have some related problems. A page on multiplying by two-digit numbers will be followed by a few problems involving multiplying by two-digit numbers. It is good that there is an opportunity to experience the mathematics in written contexts. But, one cannot assume that this knowledge will be successfully transferred to situations where the mathematics is randomly presented such as a test situation. Will the child 'recognize' the multiplication element? This is why children do less well in test situations. The time factor does not help either.

Ellen and Fiona were doing their national test for seven-year-olds. They came to a question which required mathematical knowledge they had not yet learned about but had plenty of time left. It was fascinating watching them try to solve the problem. The two of them brought many past experiences to the situation, found they did not work and tried something else. Although they did not solve the problem their approach deserved great praise. Their ability to cast around and willingness to try again when they failed was brilliant. No marks for that question on the test but, for me, the knowledge that here were two children who were resilient in their approach to mathematics was very rewarding. This persistence in the face of failure is an oft neglected part of problem solving. Too many single attempts followed by surrender are seen in the classroom with no time as an excuse to move on. As adults we sometimes spend days and months attempting to find solutions to problems. Why do we expect children to solve problems in the next five minutes and only have one attempt before providing the answer? Do we need to consider this aspect? At worst we lose a bit of time, at best we start to grow resilience in our pupils.

Additional factors which can add difficulties to successful problem solving are; problems with many words which confuse the issue by giving red herrings, multi-step calculations and the longer the calculations the more chance there is of making a mistake.

Possible ways forward

There have been several studies into how to get children to succeed at problem solving. Some advocate a lot of practise at solving similar problems. It is easy to spot that this is helpful but also has its limitations as many problems are different. It is possible that there is a false sense of success achieved when children solve problems which follow on from immediate prior practise of the calculations required.

An alternative school of thought is to provide a series of de-contextualized strategies which it is hoped can be transferred to any problem. This follows the skills or process orientated approach. Askew (2004: 116) offers three questions for problem solvers to use:

- What is the problem?
- What method of calculation should be used?
- Is it a sensible solution?

To which he adds helpful subsidiary pointers such as, 'asking children to explain in their own words', which of the four rules is most appropriate and, 'putting children in pairs to share their work'

This will probably help children to organize their approach but there is still apparent difficulty in solving the problem related to recognition of the mathematics which in turn is a transfer of prior knowledge. Whilst this is more easily identified in calculations the words and the arrangement of the order of information in word problems tend to inhibit transfer because there is: a lack of recognition, the challenge of ordering the information into a calculation and finally, as Askew notes, checking that you have a reasonable answer.

Prompts to assist solving problems

What is the question asking?

The first key to solving a problem is to establish what the question is asking. Making sense of the words is often helped by putting the question in your own words. Working with a partner enables children to articulate their thinking and through explaining they may gain a better understanding of the problem. Helpful questions for children to ask themselves are:

- What is this question saying? – Describe the problem in your own words.
  Work with a partner to discuss what the problem wants to know.
- Prior experience in like territory is going to help so children might ask:
  Have we seen anything like this before?
- Are there any clue words?
  If they have been taught to look for 'trigger' words, are there any present and, if yes, can an action be substituted and make sense?
  Are there any clues and can we see if that calculation fits with the question? (See Shells box for an example.)

Shells

5 children each have 15 shells. If they put them altogether how many shells will there be?

(Trigger word: 'altogether' indicating add or multiply.)

Can we draw it?

Sometimes it helps to sketch a diagram and plot the information. (See Boxes box for an example.)

Boxes

The capacity of a large box with a square base is 43,200 cm^3. If one side is 60 cm long, what might be the other dimensions?

(A quick sketch of the box might offer the realization that the 60 cm could be the height of the box or the base in which case a different answer is acceptable. There is more than one solution. Not all problems have single answers.)

What calculation could we try?

Having selected numbers for a calculation and appropriate action, check back to see if it fits with the question.

Will the answer to this calculation match the words in the question?

Does this solution answer the question?

Having completed the calculation, does it give a reasonable answer? Check with the question. Maybe it is only the first step of a multi-step problem.

Is this a reasonable answer?

If not, is there more to be done? (See Eggs box for an example.)

Eggs

372 eggs were packed into boxes with 12 eggs in each. Each box was sold for £4.80. How much did each egg cost and how much money did the seller make?

(In this problem two answers are required.)

Can we check?

If not sure it might be useful to work backwards to the start by reversing the functions or check by finding the solution a different way.

Do we need to check:

- by working backwards?
- by repeating the calculation?
- by doing it differently?

A worked example

Yesterday I was overdrawn at the bank by £187.85. Someone paid a cheque into my account and this morning I am £458.64 in credit. How much was the cheque worth that was paid in? [Taken from Haylock, 1995: 97]

First there is the need to establish the meaning of 'overdrawn' and 'credit'. This should indicate that the £187.85 is a negative amount and the £458.64 a positive amount.

As the cheque changed the amount from the negative to the positive we need to find out how 187.85 moves through 0 to 458.64. This requires an understanding of how negative numbers behave. A diagram might help:

$$187.85 \longrightarrow 0 \longrightarrow 458.64$$

We will need to add 187.85 to get to 0 and 458.64 to get to 458.64, so, we must add the two together to get the value of the cheque.

$$£187.85 + £458.64 = £646.49$$

Does this make sense? Back to the question, 'How much was paid in?' Yes, about 200 to bring it to 0 and another 450 to get to the current total.

If children are curious about mathematics then problem solving and creative mathematics is the ultimate joy. Even if they see it as a 'must do' subject, the application of knowledge combined with a resilience to accept failure and try again goes a long way to their becoming mathematicians rather than just learning some new mathematics. We all like to have a chance to use the skills we have learned so let's give more room to mathematical problem solving.

References

Askew, M. (2004) *Teaching Primary Mathematics*, Abingdon: Hodder and Stoughton, pp. 107–23.

Carpenter, T., Moser, J. and Romberg, T. (eds) (1982) *Addition and Subtraction: A Cognitive Perspective* (ch. 2), Hillsdale, NJ: Lawrence Erlbaum Associates.

Gelman, R. and Gallistel, C. (1978) in *The Child's Understanding of Number*, Cambridge, MA: Harvard University Press.

Gelman, R. and Gallistel, C. (1986) *The Child's Understanding of Number*, Cambridge, MA: Harvard University Press.

Ginsberg, H. (1977) *Children's Arithmetic: The Learning Process*, New York: Litton Education.

Greeno, J., Riley, M. and Gelman, R. (1984) 'Young Children's Counting and Understanding of Principles' in *Cognitive Psychology*, 16, pp. 94–143.

Haylock, D. (1995) *Mathematics Explained for Primary Teachers*, London: Paul Chapman Publishing.

Jones, L. (2003) 'The Problem with Problem Solving' in I. Thompson (ed.), *Enhancing Primary Mathematics Teaching*, Buckingham: Open University Press.

Kamii, C. (1985) *Children Re-invent Arithmetic: Implications of Piaget's Theory*, New York: Teachers College Press.

[Answers to Which is which – word problems box: Joining; Equalizing – take away; Comparison; Separating]

Difficult and Easy

Variations in a natural ability to understand and use mathematics will be a factor in children's achievement but mathematics itself has different degrees of difficulty. These challenges do not just exist as children progress through the curriculum but also some topics may be more abstract or more complex than others at any level. Also, some mathematics and mathematical methods are prone to misconceptions, particularly if children fail to grasp the ideas correctly when first introduced.

Learning, unlearning and relearning

The nature of the mind is that once something is learned incorrectly it is much harder to unlearn it and then re-establish a correct procedure. LePine et al. (2000) in a study on adaptability found that those with good cognitive structures were able to change their responses to a changing situation. Based on ideas first expressed by Schmidt et al. (1986) they confirmed that whilst with high levels of cognitive ability children can learn quickly; they also noticed that adaptability was aided by open-mindedness to experience, motivation and a creative personality.

Interestingly they also noted that whilst conscientiousness was a support to initial learning, it was a hindrance when required to relearn or adapt because it was hard to override previously learned knowledge and skills. This is worth considering when working with children in learning situations and particularly with those children whom you find have learned incorrect methods.

The nature of misconception

Misconceptions occur when children do not understand how something works. This could be because:

- the rule has been learned or remembered incorrectly
- the prior knowledge is incorrect
- the wrong knowledge has been applied.

Making a simple error in calculation such as adding up incorrectly is not a misconception unless the mistake recurs. If the calculations around it are correct then it is probably a simple mistake. A child is likely to self-correct a mistake when checking their work or during a discussion. This indicates that it is useful to allow opportunities for discussion and for getting children to develop checking strategies. It is quite hard to break a culture of hurrying to finish work and get it marked prior to moving on to the next task, but achieving this approach to learning will be a great contribution to life skills as well as children's mathematics education.

Children who have learned a rule incorrectly find it hard to unlearn the rule and re-establish the correct rule. The first learning tends to pop up and interfere with the new and time might need to be spent securing the correct rule. The initial error in learning often occurs when children experience a new mathematical method, do not understand why it works and are forced to fall back on rote learning a rule. An example from my childhood was a chant memorized for subtraction. Presented, for example, with the calculation:

43

17 –

I would say to myself, '7 from 3 won't go, borrow 1 and pay 1 back, 7 from 10 is 3, add 3 makes 6. 2 from 4 is 2.' This would give me an answer of 26 which is correct. I had no understanding of what I was doing and no teacher ever explained why it worked which is hardly surprising as it depends on introducing 10 to both the top number and the bottom number, but in such a way as to allow a smaller number to be subtracted from a larger number. As long as I worked the chant I could get the answer. Unfortunately, many children forgot part of the chant or placed the extra 10 in the wrong place, especially when dealing with calculations such as:

3000

1985 –

where if you do a traditional calculation masses of exchanging is required. (Try it for yourself.) The advantage of teaching such a method was the efficiency of the calculation. This lack of knowing why it works was a costly sacrifice for the goal of efficiency. A major aim of the National Numeracy Strategy (1999) in England was to make calculations understandable. This came at the expense of efficiency with the argument that lengthy methods could gradually be replaced by more economical calculations. However, there has always remained the pressure to head straight for the shortest method with little regard for understanding. (I feel I should point out that the 'borrow and payback' method of subtraction is no longer taught in English schools.)

Have a look at the traditional method of long division and say out loud what you are doing. Does what you say make numerical sense? The value of the numbers is completely lost and the rule is so long, it is highly possible that an error is introduced to the calculation. This method of division used to take up many hours of mathematics lessons in primary schools and the adults who experienced it are now more likely to reach for a calculator or employ an informal method to arrive at an answer. Learning a rule which is incorrectly learned or applied leaves a child with no alternative way of arriving at the answer because they have no sense of the likely answer, nor any alternative strategy to apply.

Some examples of this are shown in the Misconceptions box. Can you diagnose the children's errors? It would, of course, be best to talk with the children, but in their absence, what conclusions can you draw?

Misconceptions

$35.1 \times 10 = 350.1$	$7.6 \times 10 = 7.60$	17
		$\underline{5 \times}$
		535

$$\begin{array}{r} 33 \\ \underline{24 \times} \\ 66 \\ \underline{132} \\ 198 \end{array} \qquad \begin{array}{r} 65 \\ \underline{27 \times} \\ 35 \\ \underline{12} \\ 47 \end{array}$$

$$\begin{array}{r} 231 \\ \overline{3)\,713} \end{array} \qquad \begin{array}{r} 67r4 \\ 8)\,\overline{4860} \\ \underline{48} \\ 60 \\ \underline{56} \\ 4 \end{array}$$

Incorrect prior knowledge is harder to resolve. First, the misconception needs to be identified and then remedial action taken. It may be that only one child in the class has a particular misconception and it is a matter of tracking back to the error and relearning correctly so that the child can tackle the new learning. This requires a certain degree of vigilance and time on the part of the teacher.

There are a few situations where many children have problems. For example, have a look at the Adding a nought box.

Adding a nought

Children may have been taught to 'add a 0 when multiplying by 10'. Try these:

10×34 10×250 10×1002 10×3.5 10×62.05

Once you move into decimals this rule does not work. 'Add a nought' is easier to remember than 'move all the numbers up a column when multiplying by 10'. What's a column? Which way is up? What goes in the space? This action only starts to have meaning when children have a good grasp of place value.

Generally, short cuts can be tricky; learning without understanding may be quick but is not always reliable in the longer term as we see from the decimal example. I would argue that for misconceptions to be reduced, understanding of the behaviour of the numbers needs to be established – the why and how.

Why does base × height divided by 2 work when calculating the area of a triangle? How is this introduced to children?

Area of a triangle

Given that the area of a rectangle is length × breadth, draw a rectangle and draw one diagonal. The triangles created are clearly half the area of the rectangle (l × b ÷ 2). If you want to check, cut out the triangles and place them on top of one another.

Now draw a parallelogram, add in its shorter diagonal and two vertical lines from the ends of the diagonal to the opposite side. You will have created four triangles. Cut them out and make a rectangle. What lines on the parallelogram give you the area of the rectangle? (height and longer side)

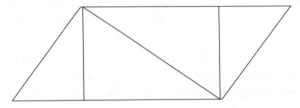

How does this help finding the area of triangles and does this work for all triangles?

Having learned and been thoroughly grooved in a vertical form of addition where first the units column is added and then the tens column plus any tens carried over from the units column, children then face a subtraction, remembering to take one number away from another. They also know that in subtraction you take the smaller number from the larger. This works well in the first example but in the second example, if the columns are treated as separate calculations, the following can happen:

$$\begin{array}{r} 28 \\ 15 \ - \\ \hline 13 \end{array} \qquad \begin{array}{r} 43 \\ 27 \ - \\ \hline 24 \end{array}$$

When the calculation is broken down into two 'mini' subtractions the value of 43 and its relation to 27 is lost. The Numeracy Strategy (DfEE, 1999) sought to remedy this misconception by strengthening mental mathematics knowledge and treating the calculation as one which could be achieved using an empty number line. One possible way would be:

43 —— less 3 —— 40 —— less —— 10 —— 30 —— less 3 —— 27

3 + 10 + 3 = 16

Although turning it around and starting at 27 might be more comfortable! To do this, children must have confidence and facility with number, otherwise it becomes just another method to learn and remember. One could argue that it leads to better understanding and therefore fewer mistakes.

Difficult mathematics

Despite efforts to provide a curriculum which builds mathematical concepts and starts from the easier mathematics and moves towards more complex mathematics, some topics seem to be harder for children to learn than others.

Numbers do not exist in the natural world, they are a language that man imposes on situations to describe the patterns in nature and those created by him. Therefore immediately children start to count they are using an abstract system and when counting objects they are relating the counting rhyme to objects in the real world. They have to understand that the number to object relationship remains constant as does the order of the numbers they are using. So we see that from the beginning children are dealing with abstract notions and these continue and grow more complex as they develop their mathematical knowledge. Viewed this way, children do remarkably well with a subject which moves from the tangible to the intangible so early on.

If there is a familiar image or action which relates to a child's mathematical learning then the knowledge will probably be established more rapidly. For example, a child used to shopping will grasp the mathematics of money very easily as they have knowledge of the coins, their value and what they are used for. A child who only goes to the supermarket with a parent who pays by credit card will probably find it harder to learn about money. Experience is an important factor in learning and if the learning is supported by related experience outside the classroom then this is a great help.

Some topics within mathematics are easier to grasp because they are easy to illustrate visually. Early counting and spatial activities such as learning about triangles, circle properties and area, have the advantage of working with images which can support oral input. This is enhanced further if children are able to manipulate the objects. The more multi-sensory the experience the more likely the learning will be established.

Measure is another topic which tends to be taught practically and can be enjoyable as well as useful. But, measure is a good example of a group of activities which can be carried out without children necessarily grasping the principles which underpin them. It is for the teacher to draw these out of the situations the children are experiencing. One drawback of working with measure is that it moves into big numbers very quickly (e.g. 1 kg = 1,000 g). Does the children's number knowledge extend this far?

Children find other mathematics topics harder to understand. Fractions are a common area of difficulty for children. They usually manage to succeed at examples with partitioned objects such as flags and cakes but stumble on the purely numerical and calculation aspects. A number line can aid the value of a fraction but the many equivalent expressions of any one fraction is confusing and calculations involving fractions are often a disaster area for children. Until they have grasped equivalence, this will remain challenging. Such knowledge depends on an awareness of 'number behaviour' and a trust that numbers will behave consistently. Gone are the supporting images when you divide a fraction by a fraction. Children have entered the world of completely abstract mathematics. The same is true when calculating with negative numbers – you have to trust them!

Decimals have also proved to be a challenging topic for children. This is mainly due to a lack of understanding of the continuation of place value below the decimal point where the numbers represent smaller and smaller parts of a whole unit. The varying length of the numbers is the main distraction. For example, order the following with the largest in value first:

3.02   3.202   3.0617   3.001

There is a tendency for children to take the quantity of numerals as their sorting criteria resulting in an order of:

3.0617   3.202   3.001   3.02

when the size of the number in the tenths column should take precedence, then the hundredth column and so on, giving an order in value of:

3.202   3.0617   3.02   3.001

Simple algebra or pre-algebra is another area of challenge. This begins very early on although x may not appear just yet. Take, for example, the following addition sums which are found in most infant (five- to seven-year olds) schools:

$$3 + 6 = \square \qquad 3 + \square = 9 \qquad \square + 6 = 9$$

One could just as easily put x in place of the box; $3 + x = 9$. You would not be surprised to find that children struggle when the box is in the first position. They have lost their starting point on the number line and in the counting rhyme and are forced to either guess or try trial and error or turn the calculation around (for which they need a grasp of commutativity). Children who decide for themselves to manipulate the calculation are well on their way to being numerate.

Word problems are challenging at any level of the mathematics curriculum. Apart from the language skills required to make sense of the initial problem, there is the decision about which mathematics to use as well as whether the numerical result answers the original question. Most problems have many 'steps' to work through and this in itself can be a problem. Multi-step calculations of any kind have the potential for error. For children, there is often a lot to remember.

When working from a syllabus or curriculum it is worth considering how difficult or easy the mathematics is going to be. People have tried to distribute the difficult mathematics higher up the syllabus but society and politicians hold strong views of what should be taught by certain ages and a move from these traditions is seen as a retrograde step. It is accepted that all teachers have to work within set parameters but in understanding why a topic is challenging will help them respond to children's difficulties. Consider whether the maths is abstract, complex, is built on previous learning, whether the children have incorrect knowledge or are just struggling with too many new concepts at one go. How can you lead them gradually and confidently forward?

Mathematically high attaining children?

Some children find mathematics very easy. They learn quickly and remember past topics. They seem to have, as Gardner (1983) claims, a talent for the subject. From the able to the gifted, what is it they can do and what are their needs? In a report by the English government (Curriculum and Standards, 2000) a closer examination of able children found that:

Pupils who are able in mathematics:

- generalise patterns and relationships and approaches to problem solving;
- are persistent and flexible in their search for solutions;
- develop logical arguments, often taking valid short cuts;
- use mathematical symbols confidently;
- rapidly grasp new material;
- may not be exceptional in carrying out calculations, but may see calculation as detail and less important than the problem as a whole.

Curriculum and Standards, p. 2

The teacher's dilemma is whether to move them on to harder mathematics or explore the present mathematics in more challenging contexts. Reflecting on the above list it would seem appropriate to get able mathematicians to exercise their inquiry and problem-solving skills in a variety of challenging contexts. By gradually removing the usual single step support structures, encouraging independence but discussing problem-solving strategies these children can be challenged in most mathematical topics. As they grasp new material quickly it would be appropriate to reduce the 'practise' skills and move sooner into the problem contexts.

The Office for Standards in Education (Ofsted, 2001) suggested that teachers working with able children should have:

- a high degree of subject knowledge
- an understanding of how to plan classwork and homework in order to increase the pace, breadth or depth of the coverage of the subject
- the capacity to envisage and organise unusual projects and approaches which catch pupils' attention and make them want to explore the topic
- the use of tasks which help pupils to develop perseverance and independence in learning through their own research or investigation, while ensuring that they have the necessary knowledge and skills to tackle the work effectively on their own
- the use of demanding resources which help pupils to engage with difficult or complex ideas
- the use of ICT to extend and enhance pupils' work and the opportunity to present the outcomes to others
- the ability to deploy high-level teaching skills in defining expectations, creating a positive classroom climate for enquiry, asking probing questions, managing time and resources, and assessing progress through the lesson

- the confidence to try out new ideas, to take risks and to be prepared to respond to leads which look most likely to develop higher levels of thinking by pupils.

Ofsted, p. 25

Difficult or easy or anywhere in-between; children vary in their speed and ability to understand mathematics but also mathematics itself can be difficult or easy to understand. By being aware of each child's grasp of the topics and by presenting the mathematics in an enjoyable, multi-sensory way, with suitable contexts and an appropriate balance of practise and application, the teacher can maximize children's opportunities to be successful learners. Realizing why a topic is difficult goes a long way to understanding how it is best taught.

References

Curriculum and Standards, Excellence in Schools (January 2000) *National Literacy and Numeracy Strategies: Guidance on Teaching Able Children*, London: DfEE, available at http://dera.ioe.ac.uk/4846/1/LNGT%20DfES.pdf (accessed September 2014).

Department for Education and Employment (DfEE) (1999) *The National Numeracy Strategy Framework for Teaching Mathematics from Reception to Year 6*, London: DfEE.

Gardner, H. (1983) *Frames of Mind: The Theory of Multiple Intelligences*, New York: Basic Books.

LePine, J., Colquitt, J. and Erez, A. (2000) 'Adaptability to Changing Task Contexts: Effects of General Cognitive Ability, Conscientiousness, and Openness to Experience' in *Personnel Psychology*, 53:3, pp. 563–93.

Ofsted (2001) *Providing for Gifted and Talented Pupils: An Evaluation of Excellence in Cities and Other Grant-Funded Programmes*, December 2001, HMI 334, available at http://dera.ioe.ac.uk/4528/1/giftedandtalented.pdf (accessed June 2015).

Schmidt, F., Hunter, J. and Outerbridge, A. (1986) 'Impact of Job Experience and Ability on Job Knowledge, Work Sample Performance, and Supervisory Ratings of Job Performance' in *Journal of Applied Psychology*, 71, pp. 432–39.

13

Relationships, Patterns and Generalization

Mathematics is more than a set of calculations. If children can see the relationships which underpin the mathematics they will be able to see similarities, apply known mathematics to new situations and be able to create their own mathematics. Patterns, relationships and generalization are key elements in becoming a functioning mathematician.

Relationships

A relationship is about how one thing behaves towards another. If this behaviour is consistent then it becomes an established relationship. $6 \div 2$ is always 3. This relationship is consistent and can be relied upon to always produce an answer of 3. There are several relationships between the numbers 12, 4 and 3 involving $\times$ and $\div$ which I am sure you can describe. These relationships can be described more generally; two smaller numbers (factors) can be multiplied to give a larger number (multiple) and a multiple divided by a factor will give another factor. This statement is always true for whole numbers so can be called a 'generalization' because it applies to all situations involving factors and multiples. This is useful as it is transferable. If 24 is a multiple of 8 and 3 we can therefore assume that $24 \div 3 = 8$ and $24 \div 8 = 3$ and, if 132 has a pair of factors of 12 and 11 then $132 \div 12 = 11$ and $132 \div 11 = 12$. It is good to discuss the relationships between numbers as it can lead to broader understanding and application.

The Exploring common mathematical relationships box shows some common relationships which primary school children experience and are expected to know. The interesting question is why do they work? It is, of course, possible to just learn some of these relationships but understanding why is probably more memorable and more useful. When looking for relationships start with easy numbers so that children can concentrate on what is happening and then get them to test their theory with other numbers.

Exploring common mathematical relationships

Angles of a triangle add up to 180°. Before revealing this, try drawing some triangles with different numbers and see what happens (e.g. a triangle with angles of 40°, 70° and 90°).

All numbers divisible by 5 end in 5 or 0. Before revealing this, use the calculator to generate multiples of 5. Spot the pattern.

6/10 can be expressed as 0.6. Is this true for all fractions with a denominator of 10? Recognizing that / can be ÷, try other tenths on the calculator. What happens with 100 as the denominator?

Diagonally opposite angles of a parallelogram are equal. Is this true and if so why? Are there other quadrilaterals where this is true? (Geo Strips are useful in exploring this relationship.)

1/8 is 0.125 as a decimal (1 ÷ 8). What is 2/8 as a decimal? Can you predict what 3/8 will be as a decimal? Is there an eighths pattern? What about other fraction to decimal conversions? (Beware the calculators rounding action when the digits fill the screen.)

A square has a rotational symmetry order of 4. What is the rotational symmetry order of an equilateral triangle? What about a scalene triangle? Try more shapes with a different number of sides? Can you find a rule? (The rule of number of sides = order of rotation will only work when the sides are the same length – are regular shapes.)

An odd number added to an odd number always gives an even number answer. Is this true? What about even + even or even + odd? Why is this so? (Cubes are useful in illustrating why.)

The calculator is used to generate calculations easily so that attention can be focused on the patterns.

It is reassuring for children if they can 'see' a relationship. For example, speed equals distance over time. They can memorize $s = d/t$ and hope that they can recall the order of the letters. Some additional preliminary work with simple numbers can help to explain what is happening but also gives an additional memory to boost correct recall. For example, if a car travels 60 km in 1 hour its speed will be $s = 60/1$ or 60 km per hour (60 km/h). If a child is not sure of the arrangement of the formula it would be possible to rework this example to reassure them they have the letters in the right position before moving on to the current problem. It is these additional memories that can reassure and support the mathematics. It is having a backup example to enable the child to check that he or she is right. This illustrates the value of practise but also of simplicity of numbers in drawing out the relationship which is the aspect that will need to be remembered and transferred. They might be regarded as a collection of example prompts – the backup plan!

Patterns

Patterns in mathematics are not only found in numbers and shapes behaving in a consistent way but also provide sequences which can be mathematically described. For example, in the sequence 2, 4, 6, 8 ... the function which generates the sequence is +2. The sequence 1, 3, 5, 7 also has a function of +2, it just starts in a different place. In the sequence 1, 2, 4, 8, 16 the function is doubling. Similar descriptions can be applied to shapes such as snowflakes have a function of rotating 60° creating an order of rotation of 6. A square turns 90° giving it a rotational order of 4 whilst a parallelogram has a rotational order of 2 or 180°.

Young children initially see pattern as repeats (Sangster, 2000). They also see the counting sequence 1, 2, 3, 4 ... as a pattern but they have yet to see the relationship which holds it together, the +1. This is not surprising as it is hidden. After a while they learn about addition but it is rarely related to pattern generation until much later when children are asked to find the rule which forms a sequence. Sequences such as 24, 30, 36, 42 . . . or 24, 19, 14, 9 . . . can be a relatively easy challenge but does require children to see what comes in-between the numbers. Even later in secondary school (11–16 years) more complex sequences are experienced with multi-functions and complex rules expressed in algebraic form. But the roots of that algebra, pre-algebra as some would call it are found in the primary school.

Pattern-seeking skills

From the literature on problem solving it can be seen that pattern seeking is considered by many to be an important element in investigating and solving problems in mathematics (Burton, 1984; Mason et al., 1986; Garrard, 1986; Bird, 1991; Orton and Frobisher, 1996). Many mathematical situations can be understood and predictions made, once the underlying structure is realized and a rule established for continuance. Mason et al. (1986) describe successful pattern searching as having two essential elements; prior knowledge experience which can be used in a new situation and, being prepared to search actively for the presence of a pattern. In searching for pattern, mental processes occur which appear to range from simple recognition to sophisticated application of property features.

Pattern seeking requires a range of strategies and persistence. The persistence comes from interest, curiosity and time to try things out. It should be acceptable to fail and then try a different strategy. How often does primary mathematics offer children the opportunity to exercise these skills? With a curriculum crammed with knowledge and calculation methods it is hard to create space for exploration and application. Surely we would not wish to deny children the opportunity to use the mathematics they have learned? There are several aspects to how children respond to patterns. They may be able to recognize a pattern, they may be able to describe how it works and therefore be able to continue it. Additionally, they may be able to create their own patterns with a consistent rule. Later on this rule may be described using algebraic notation.

It is not a simple process. When children move beyond learning a sequence such as even numbers in the same way they learn the spelling of a word, many skills are required. When Bird (1991) observed five- and six-year-olds at work on problem solving, she amassed a list of ninety-six skills and strategies which she considered the children had used. Some of the skills she observed were: searching for/finding patterns and relationships, conjecturing, extrapolating, manipulating, deciding on rules, recognizing equivalence, patterning, generalizing, using rules, transforming, classifying, structuring and comparing. Orton and Frobisher (1996) provide an interesting diagram on processes in investigation at a secondary school level drawn from Frobisher's earlier work in 1994. They are describing the aim of mathematical problem solving. It should be to develop 'knowledge of the relationships which exist between mathematical processes, as the one leads naturally into another' (p. 38). Their diagrammatic representation of this process is reproduced:

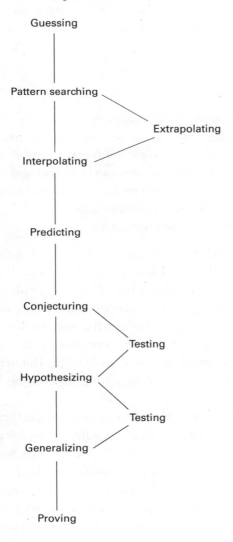

Orton and Frobisher, p. 38

As you can see the actions are remarkably similar to Bird's findings with young children and Garrard's (1986) in her research of young children (five-to six-year-olds). She drew up a list of procedures which holds true even for adults seeking patterns. She refers to 'getting started' in which children need to work out what the question is asking, 'mulling over' in which they are thinking rather than acting, 'coming up with a question' and trying to think things through. Next they 'look for a pattern', find a possible one and 'see if it works'. And then there is the 'recording' and 'explaining to others' what they have done and what they have found out. Finally there might be a phase where they see if their pattern works in another situation. This last action is a move towards transfer and generalization.

Generalizing

An important part of understanding mathematics is knowing when something, within reason, 'always happens' and can be transferred to many new situations. This is called generalizing. Whilst generalizing is a recognized feature of later mathematics, primary school children can be encouraged to think in this way. Much of the development of generalizing will lie in the questions and focus that the teacher chooses to communicate.

Two simple examples taken from early mathematics are:

- When counting, the next number in the sequence is always 1 more (+1). The next even number will be 2 more than the previous one. If n is even then n + 2 will be even. Is this always true? Give an example of an even number and add 2. Do you get the next even number? How do you know it is even? (Cubes can help to illustrate that even numbers are exactly divisible by 2.) This example may be very obvious but it is the relationship that is being pointed out; the 'always'. Getting children to think in this way could be described as getting them to be a mathematician.

- If all the class were each to draw a triangle and measure the angles they will find they usually add up to 180°. It would be possible to propose **a theory** that the angles of all triangles add up to 180° but you have **not proved** it. That would require a **geometric proof** such as the angles of a triangle being half that of a quadrilateral but then why do angles of a quadrilateral add up to 360°? Eventually you work your way back to Euclid and his axioms and proofs where some basic principles are agreed. A **general statement** is about things which are normally predictable and can be transferred with the expectation that the mathematics will behave in the same way. By the way, if you plot a triangle on a curved surface the sum of the angles is greater than 180°; hence the use of the words normally and usually!

How do we teach children to think in this way? Most of it is about having the right conversations and questions such as: 'Does that always happen?', 'Can you think of another example?', 'Where else have you seen this happening?' and, 'Can we use that idea here?' Bills et al. (2004) recommend a process called Particular, Peculiar, General (PPG) in which they ask the children to give a particular example such as a fraction equivalent of 0.2. This might be 2/10, then a peculiar example which might be 250/1250 and then a general example which could be expressed as n/5n where the denominator is always 5 times bigger than the numerator. In this way the underlying relationship between numerator and denominator is revealed. Try a PPG with your class.

References

Bills, C., Bills, L., Watson, A. and Mason, J. (2004) *Thinkers*, Derby: Association of Teachers of Mathematics (ATM).

Bird, M. (1991) *Mathematics for Young Children: An Active Thinking Approach*, London: Routledge.

Burton, L. (1984) *Thinking Things Through*, Oxford: Blackwell.

Frobisher, L. (1994) 'Problems, Investigations and Investigative Approach', ch. 10 in A. Orton and G. Wain (eds) *Issues in Teaching Mathematics*, London: Cassell.

Garrard, W. (1986) *I don't know, let's find out*, Leicester: Mathematical Association (MA).

Mason, J., Burton, L. and Stacey, K. (1986) *Thinking Mathematically*, London: Addison-Wesley.

Orton, A. and Frobisher, L. (1996) *Insights into Teaching Mathematics*, London: Cassell.

Orton, A. and Wain, G. (eds) (1994) *Issues in Teaching Mathematics*, London: Cassell.

Sangster, M. (2000) *An Exploration of Pattern in the Primary School*, PhD (unpublished) Roehampton University.

Part IV

The Teacher's Influence on Children Learning Primary Mathematics

14

The Nature of Mathematical Knowledge for Teaching

There was a time when it was believed that if you were good at mathematics then you would be a good teacher of mathematics. There is no denying that an appropriate level of subject knowledge is required to teach. This is much clearer at university and secondary school level (11 to 16 years) than it is in the primary school (5 to 11 years). Lee Shulman (1986) brought about a change of perspective when he wrote about effective mathematics teaching:

> No one asked how subject matter was transformed from the knowledge of the teacher into the content of instruction. Nor did they ask how particular formulations of that content related to what students came to know or misconstrue (even though the question had become the central query of cognitive research on learning).
>
> Shulman, p. 4

He proposed a theory where mathematics teaching was split into different types of knowledge: content knowledge, pedagogic knowledge and curriculum knowledge, and many subdivisions of these three. Whilst this model broadened people's thinking about teaching mathematics it is not always easy to discern which is in action when teaching.

Since Shulman many people have provided empirical research on his three components, particularly the pedagogic content knowledge (PCK). Depaepe et al. (2013) summarize much of this research in their literature review. In their introduction they reflect on the possible nature of PCK developing from Shulman's two main components; knowledge of instructional strategies and students' misconceptions in which he included knowledge of useful representation, illustration and demonstration, explanation, analogy and awareness of pupils' prior knowledge (Shulman 1986: 8/9). Depaepe et al.'s findings suggest Schulman's theories are still a 'hot topic' for research. Ball et al. (2008) have carried out extensive enquiries in this area and prefer the term Mathematics Teaching Knowledge (MTK). However the main development in recent years is the split between those who believe PCK can be learned 'cold' and those who feel it is a situated application of knowledge, a 'knowing-to-act' which is embedded in teacher beliefs and decision making as well as the knowledge of how one might act (Petrou and Goulding, 2011).

Another series of studies which has made an exploration of teachers' actions in primary school mathematics lessons is that of Huckstep et al. (2003). Twenty-four video tapes of primary postgraduate students teaching maths on their final practice were studied in depth. Using grounded theory, the tapes were analyzed and eighteen aspects of practice were produced. These were later grouped into four themes: foundation, transformation, connection and contingency (Rowland et al., 2003), which they called the 'Knowledge Quartet'. As further observations are made of primary school mathematics teaching it is clear it is a complex mix of mathematical knowledge, general teaching strategies, knowledge of good ways to impart mathematical ideas, an awareness of the 'bigger picture' of the mathematics and teachers' own beliefs about how mathematics should be taught. And that list does not include how schools and parents think mathematics should be taught.

Liping Ma (2010) caused a sensation when she compared American elementary school teachers with those in China. She found the American teachers far less knowledgeable about mathematics but also concluded that, 'To facilitate learning, teachers tend to make explicit the connections between and among mathematics topics that remain tacit for non-teachers' (p. 21). This echoes the work of Askew et al. (1997) who also concluded:

> What would appear to matter in relation to the effectiveness of teachers is not formal qualifications or the amount of formal subject knowledge, but the nature of the knowledge about the subject that teachers have. The

connectedness of teachers' mathematical knowledge in terms of their appreciation of the multi-faceted nature of mathematical meanings does appear to be a factor associated with greater pupil learning gains.

Askew et al., p. 93

At the same time Nola (1997) published her work on depths of teacher knowledge. She described six types of knowing which could provide a prompt for thinking about depth of teacher's and children's mathematical understanding. Paraphrased they are:

1   A person knows a direct object.
2   A person knows how to do something.
3   A person knows how to explain.
4   A person knows why something works.
5   A person knows that something happens.
6   A person knows what something is.

Nola, p. 62

Take a piece of knowledge such as giving a 20 per cent reduction to an item in a sale. Which of Nola's types of knowing can you say yes to? It seems that points 3 and 4 are the specific concern of teachers. Being able to explain, not just how to do a calculation but also why it works; to even have an alternative way of explaining it when a child does not understand, is an important skill of a teacher and to do this requires a depth of understanding beyond being able to successfully apply and complete a calculation. Prior to teaching that is all that has been required – a distilled memory of a single successful method. Whilst this is efficient and functional in the adult world, teaching asks more of its teachers – a pedagogic knowledge of strategies which can enable effective communication with all the learners in their care.

Teacher beliefs

The idea of teacher choices and beliefs is more recent research territory but possibly a very fruitful one. Beliefs can be a very strong driver of actions. A cynical view of teaching is that people, no matter what they have experienced in training, will revert when teaching to the way they were taught. This could possibly be true if they have no other strategy or they believe their own success was due to the way they were taught. This is why it is so important to experience a range of different teaching styles and have the opportunity to discuss their effectiveness. Teaching style is underpinned by a personal belief in how to teach. A nice illustration can be found in Escudero and Sanchez's study of two secondary (11 to 16 years) school teachers (2007). Although about secondary teachers there is no reason to see why it should not apply to primary teachers too. They noted that the two teachers responded to context, socio-cultural and situated aspects of their lessons but in their summary they described each teacher's actions as embedded in their belief about how mathematics should be taught:

> Ismael held an approach to teaching that emphasized that students come to see mathematical ideas and relationships through their own experience. For him, to teach was to provide students situations that would allow them to reveal mathematical meanings. In addition to this, he integrated his knowledge about learning as an active process of discovering of mathematical ideas through those situations. He also included knowledge about learners' ideas, difficulties and previous knowledge. Furthermore, he incorporated a view of school mathematics in which ideas were interconnected, emphasizing the understanding of concepts, especially with respect to procedures. His subject matter knowledge led Ismael to give great significance to the establishment of numerical/geometrical connections by means of selected problems.
>
> The second teacher, Juan, considered teaching as an attempt to provide information about particular mathematical ideas to students. His way of knowing the learning processes was integrated with the use of sequential steps as a means of facilitating students' learning. In addition, he tried to pre-empt all foreseen difficulties related to low level and lack of motivation in his previous planning decisions, admitting the verification as an easier procedure for the introduction of the content. Juan's algorithm approach to the content of the instructional unit was associated with a more general view of school mathematics.
>
> Escudero and Sanchez, p. 325

Returning to one of the PCK studies we see something similar emerging. Mansor et al. (2010) in their enquiry into pedagogic content knowledge found that an important element of effective pupil learning was the eagerness and earnestness of the teacher. They concluded that, 'appropriate teachers' attitudes and emotions coupled with effective PCK will ensure learning takes place' (p. 1837). This might be rather a definitive statement but the idea of the teacher's emotional approach to the subject being a strong influence is one which has recently come under closer examination. One could argue that teacher training is more than the acquisition of skills and knowledge and that there is a strong personal development element which contributes to good teaching. Evans' (2011) work indicates this when she describes 'the "real" shape of teacher professionalism will be that that teachers forge for themselves' (p. 868), a conclusion she draws from her analysis of 'enacted' and 'demanded' professionalism. This 'broader professionalism' is also identified by Malm (2009) when she suggests that good teachers draw upon their intellectual, social and emotional experiences.

As Brown (2005) indicates, we are the sum total of our experiences to date and these may have been variable in learning mathematics. This could involve several changes of philosophy which presents a confusing picture. A teacher may have experienced several styles of mathematics teaching and will have a degree of faith in a style that worked for them. How does a student make sense of the maths they have experienced at school, possibly a different way of teaching maths in the university and then on placements where different approaches may again be presented to them? From this range of experience each student must forge their own ideology of maths and must operate it within the confines of the settings they find themselves in. This requires a degree of metacognitive awareness of one's beliefs and style and a reasonable level of confidence in those beliefs.

This view is endorsed by Walshaw (2004) who claims that student teachers' identities are constantly being challenged and that a classroom is not a comfortable place to be but a setting where 'constant social negotiation' (p. 65) takes place between the class teacher and the student. Further, Walshaw describes this as a play of 'power relations' between the student teacher's ideological university view and the actual practice and expectations of the class teacher. Pepperell's (2007) study of one student's move to their first teaching post indicates that new learning from initial teacher education courses may not be as secure as hoped when moving into the school environment of their first teaching post. Possibly the easiest route, in such a new and intimidating environment is to continue current school practice. It appears that school settings on practice or in first posts can have a more powerful influence than previously recognized. This could equally be applied throughout a teaching career to the relationship between teacher and school expectations.

Self-concept and confidence

Self-concept of how good you are at mathematics underpins the level of confidence you have in your mathematics ability. If you talk to young children they will tell you whether they enjoy mathematics, are any good at it and will display how willing they are to tackle mathematical tasks. From an early age they are probably aware of their position in class and Landers (2003) found traces of maths anxiety with children as young as five. Self-concept of mathematical ability will be present throughout formal education. It will depend on position and achievement. Student teachers bring a sense of their mathematical ability into teacher training courses and from there, into the classroom. This self-concept is derived from their success or failure with their personal mathematics. The more good experiences a student teacher has in the classroom, the more their confidence grows in their ability to teach mathematics. In terms of confidence to teach, there is evidence (Sangster, 2008, 2012) that personal mathematics ability, in many cases, drives students' confidence to teach, particularly when some of those with good grades felt they could teach very young children and some of those with lower grades were not confident in teaching ten- and eleven-year-olds. However, it would be dangerous to assume that this was true for all student teachers. Confidence is a delicate flower and easily destroyed. Success in the classroom undoubtedly boosts confidence and I would suggest, leads to greater engagement which in turn will probably lead to greater pupil learning.

It is important that teachers cast a critical eye over their own teaching and the teaching of others so that they can develop their own belief about effective mathematics teaching. From this chapter we can see that teacher knowledge is a complex mix of knowing the mathematics, knowing how to explain it well, having a range of strategies to support teaching and a deep understanding of how the mathematics works at an appropriate level. Added to this is the confidence to teach and an enthusiasm for the subject. Alexander in his report on primary education (2010: 408) describes a good teacher bringing both 'head and heart' to their teaching.

References

Alexander, R. (2010) *Children Their World, Their Education*, Abingdon: Routledge.

Askew, M., Brown, M., Rhodes, V., Johnson, D. and Wiliam, D. (1997) *Effective Teachers of Numeracy*, London: King's College.

Ball, D., Hoover, M. and Phelps, G. (2008) 'Content Knowledge for Teaching: What Makes It Special?' in *Journal of Teacher Education*, 59:5, pp. 389–407.

Brown, T. (2005) 'The Truth of Initial Training Experiences in Maths for Primary Teachers' in *Day Proceedings of the British Society of Research for Learning in Mathematics* 25:2, Open University (June 2005).

Depaepe, F., Verschaffel, L. and Kelchtermans, G. (2013) 'Pedagogical Content Knowledge: A Systematic Review of the Way in Which the Concept has Pervaded Mathematics Educational Research' in *Teaching and Teacher Education*, 34, pp. 12–25.

Escudero, I. and Sanchez, V. (2007) 'How Do Domains of Knowledge Integrate Into Mathematics Teachers' Practice?' in *Journal of Mathematical Behavior*, 26, pp. 312–27.

Evans, L. (2011) 'The "Shape" of Teacher Professionalism in England: Professional Standards, Performance Management, Professional Development and Changes Proposed in the 2010 White Paper' in *British Educational Research Journal*, Vol. 37:5 (October 2011), pp. 851–70.

Huckstep, P., Rowland, T. and Thwaites, A. (2003) 'Primary Teachers' Mathematical Content Knowledge: What Does It Look Like In The Classroom?' in *Education-Line* http://www.leeds.ac.uk/educol/documents/00002534.htm (accessed January 2015).

Landers, J. (2003) 'Mathematics Anxiety in the Primary School', MA thesis (unpublished), Sheffield Hallam University.

Ma, L. (2010) (anniversary edition) *Knowing and Teaching Elementary Mathematics*, Routledge: Abingdon.

Malm, B. (2009) 'Towards a New Professionalism: Enhancing Personal and Professional Development in Teacher Education' in *Journal of Education for Teaching*, Vol. 35:1 (February 2009), pp. 77–91.

Mansor, R., Halim, L. and Osman, K. (2010) 'Teachers' Knowledge that Promote Students' Conceptual Understanding' in *Procedia Social and Behavioural Sciences*, 9 (pp. 1835–9), available at www.sciencedirect.com (accessed January 2015).

Nola, R. (1997) 'Constructivism in Science and Science Education: A Philosophical Critique' in *Science and Education*, 6:1–2, pp. 55–83.

Pepperell, S. (2007) 'An Examination of the Developing Maths Teaching Practices of Primary Teachers from Initial Teacher Education into First Teaching Posts' in *Day Proceedings of the British Society for Research into the Learning of Maths*, London South Bank (March 2007).

Petrou, M. and Goulding, M. (2011) 'Conceptualising Teachers' Mathematical Knowledge in Teaching' in T. Rowland and K. Ruthven (eds), *Mathematical Knowledge in Teaching*, pp. 9–25, Dordrecht: Springer.

Rowland, T., Huckstep, P. and Thwaites, A. (2003) 'The Knowledge Quartet' in *Day Proceedings of the British Society for Research into the Learning of Maths*, Birmingham (November 2003).

Sangster, M. (2008) 'What is the Nature of the Link Between Students' Mathematical Qualification, Subject Knowledge and their Confidence to Teach Primary Mathematics' in *Day Proceedings of the British Society for Research into the Learning of* Maths 28:2, University of Southampton (June 2008), pp. 97–102.

Sangster, M. (2012) 'A Further Study of the Nature of the Link Between Students' Mathematics Qualification and their Confidence in their Subject Knowledge and Confidence to Teach Primary Mathematics', Presentation at BSRLM day conference, London University (unpublished).

Shulman, L. (1986) 'Those Who Understand: Knowledge Growth in Teaching' in *Educational Researcher* 15 (February 1986), pp. 4–14.

Walshaw, M. 2004. 'Pre-service Maths Teaching in the Context of Schools: An Exploration into the Constitution of Identity' in *Journal of Maths Teacher Education* 7, pp. 63–86.

15

Creating a Good Learning Environment

As a teacher one would hope to create a learning environment which is stimulating and motivating, exciting and inclusive, comfortable but challenging, where knowledge is accessible. This is a demanding list in which success is built upon the relationship between the teacher and the children in his or her care. As Pointon and Kershner (2000) say, '[E]very classroom is a complex and changing environment that requires creative and decisive day-to-day management by teachers' (p. 117). A successful learning environment is hard to evidence but it must be a mix of many factors. For example, the physical environment which includes how the class seating is organized, what is on the walls, the type of tasks and the time allocated to them. It is also dependent on the social and emotional environment which includes the relationships between pupils and between teacher and pupils as well as how they are expected to work together. And then, there are also the expectations; the rules and routines, the values being promoted and the goals being set. The teacher makes nearly all of these decisions based on their belief about what their classroom should be, creating a classroom culture to support learning.

Teacher input

The teacher is the best instructional element in the lesson because he or she can respond to the children – interact, clarify, give appropriate examples and listen to explanations. The teacher can manage the input and tasks so that they are inclusive but also challenging. The teacher also sets the ethos of the classroom. Is it a place where children can speak out without fear of peer mockery? Do children ask questions? Do children set their own exploratory questions? Are they able to pursue enquiry mathematics over a more extended period of time than a single lesson?

It is worth considering the research of Huckstep et al. (2003) and Rowland et al. (2003) again. Their observation of teachers in primary mathematics lessons led to the creation of eighteen codes or actions about what the teacher does:

- anticipation of complexity
- identifying errors
- awareness of purpose
- making connections
- adherence to the text book
- overt subject knowledge
- choice of examples
- recognition of conceptual appropriateness
- concentration on procedures
- responding to children's ideas
- choice of representation
- theoretical underpinning
- deviation from agenda
- use of opportunities
- demonstration
- use of terminology
- decisions about sequencing
- demonstration.

These are skills which teachers need. For example, it is important that a teacher chooses a good example to show children how the mathematics works. A really good explanation or illustration comes from preparation. Trying to find a good illustration of a fraction divided by a fraction is a notoriously difficult piece of mathematics to illustrate whilst addition has many real world examples. Gradually teachers build up a store of effective explanations as they see which examples the children respond to.

Interestingly, newer teachers tend to keep to the 'script' of their lesson. This might be due to a lack of confidence or a lack of alternative routes as yet. Experienced teachers are more relaxed about being 'diverted' and spending short amounts of time pursuing comments and questions made by the children. This can be good if it is relevant to the mathematics and enables greater enlightenment for the class. However, diversions can 'slow' the lesson down and children can become restless as attention focusses on one child. It is about making the decisions that maintain the balance between class engagement and the learning taking place. Alexander (2010) refers to this as the pace of the lesson:

> The pace that matters in a classroom is 'interactive pace' ('the pace of teacher-pupil and pupil-pupil exchanges, and contingent factors such as maintaining focus and handling cues and turns'), 'cognitive pace' ('the speed at which conceptual ground is covered') and 'learning pace' ('how fast pupils actually learn'). The critical issue . . . has to be the relationship of interactive pace to cognition and learning' and international research shows how a more studied interactive pace, with longer teacher-pupil exchanges, is more effective cognitively than the rapid fire sequence of brief exchange . . .
>
> Alexander, p. 295

The quality and nature of questioning is a further key element to effective teaching and this is addressed more extensively in Chapter 17. The teacher is a major element of a successful mathematics lesson but there is also a 'supporting cast' such as the materials used, the classroom environment and other adults working with individual children and small groups.

Resources and displays

In England the classroom environment has traditionally been colourful, well resourced and busy. Computers, overhead projectors and access to the internet have made the classroom one of the most potentially stimulating school environments for children in the world. Is this a good thing? Some would argue it is not, that it is distracting and lacking in focus. Others would say this is fine for young children but not necessary as they grow older (Smith and Call, 1999). I find this statement difficult to agree with. One of the most successful sixth form classrooms I entered was full of interesting mathematical posters as was a very successful university department.

To me, a wealth of resources is an opportunity but it is an opportunity which must be managed if particular learning is to take place. Play is valuable and is a major part of establishing ideas and connections in the children's minds but, as always, there is a balance between play and a more focussed learning style where, through teacher direction, new ideas can be experienced. It is for the teacher to decide what learning each activity or resource is supporting and when it is appropriate to sit back and watch what the children do. As a facilitator, the teacher is directing children's attention to the learning, either directly or indirectly, through questioning and comment.

Computer programs and internet resources are a great way of bringing the outside world into the classroom. For mathematics there are many practice programs which children enjoy. There are a few puzzle programs too. There are short films and images which show mathematics in ways teachers' cannot possibly produce in the classroom.

There are a range of display types, each of which can be used for promoting mathematics as much as any other subject. A display might be of good work done. It might be an informative display of an up-and-coming topic – a wetting of the appetite. It might be an interactive display such as folding the nets of shapes or creating a block graph with cubes. It might be a challenge such as asking how many cats were on the way to St Ives in the nursery rhyme 'I met a man on the way to St Ives'. It might be a contributory task such as the three little bears had three hats, three coats and three scarves between them. How many different ways could they dress? Using blank pictures of the bears, add a different outfit to the display. Or, with the cost of eight items for a lunch box, show the different lunch boxes you could pack with four items and their total cost.

There are, with any contributory displays, issues of self-esteem to consider. Has everyone contributed? What is the quality of the contribution? These things matter to children. It is like 'going public' which can be a nervous and sometimes unkind experience but also it can be a very rewarding one. Muijs and Reynolds (2005) refer to the pride in having one's work displayed. Children can also have a pride in how their classroom looks, especially when parents are the audience. How involved have they been in deciding what goes up on the walls? (Price, 2013). The affective aspect of the class as a group is a strong contributor to the success of the learning environment.

Other environments

Can you have mathematical visits? Yes you can! It is not usual to plan a school visit based on mathematics but there are places which can be a good source for mathematical thinking. What are the advantages of leaving the classroom to do some mathematics? Like any school visit or working away from the classroom, it is memorable (Carver, 2003), it can be a rich stimulus and provide resources for meaningful follow-up work. It also provides a context for learning and as such is more likely to be remembered. It provides an opportunity to apply mathematics in real situations. Scoffham and Barnes (2010) consider that the positive emotions generated by visits can impact positively on children's learning. Green (2013) explores why working outside the classroom is beneficial to children's learning as well as their motivation and well-being. Look at the Some mathematics outside the classroom box for examples of mathematical activities suitable for either just outside the classroom or on visits.

Some mathematics outside the classroom

- Visit the supermarket to consider price comparisons, probability of sale in relation to product shelving, turnover, types of goods purchased, surveys of customers.
- Survey different plants and animals in 10 square centimetres of grass.
- Go to the graveyard to look at dates of death, numbers of deaths related to year, comparison with census records and historical events.
- Collect car number plates and looking at frequency of letters and numerals.
- Record creatures found in pond dipping samples.
- Survey frequency of types of traffic where it would be good to have a pedestrian crossing.
- Work out the water speed of a stream.
- Count the number of birds seen on a short walk.
- Survey the types and frequency of birds visiting the bird table.
- Design a symmetrical pattern on clay tiles after a visit to the tile making factory or DIY store.

Some of these can be pursued in the school grounds. It is worth including a mathematical task in any general visit if it is appropriate.

Task type

Traditionally, in England, there was a time when children did mental mathematics tests and then worked through text books or workbooks. The text books were structured in a form of distance learning, a way that children could progress without the help of the teacher unless they got into difficulties. As the books were written by someone who had no knowledge of the children in the class they were pitched generally at an age group. Successful children worked their way through book after book whilst those who struggled barely finished each page. Most of the books were structured in the same way, an introduction and modelling of the topic, a practise section, usually numerical in nature, followed by some word problems. There was little practical activity or if there was, it was often bypassed by the teacher as messy, noisy and probably required equipment that they had not got. Since those days things have progressed with more practical work and more teaching of the class or groups within the class.

Have the tasks improved over time and the introduction of many curricula? I am not so sure. There is still a need for models or examples, for practise and for application. Maybe it is the balance of these three which has changed. There seems to be more opportunities for application with more practical tasks present in lessons. Also teachers have made the tasks more relevant to the children they are teaching by choosing realistic or interesting contexts. The modelling is normally done by the teacher in a discussion with the children. Still, a key area is the dialogue which develops understanding of the mathematics which needs to be remembered and is potentially transferable to new situations. As discussed earlier, this transfer is embedded in practising in a range of contexts and identifying the key mathematical elements. This is something effective teachers draw out of the tasks as children work or once they have completed them. It is good to remember to talk the maths rather than talk the task.

If children are to be motivated and engaged then tasks need to be pitched at a level where children can get started on them and want to start because they look interesting. This depends on the teacher knowing the level at which the children are operating and what context might interest them. Reality, puzzles and practical activities each make engaging tasks. Is there a way you can turn the usual task into a more captivating one?

Twisting the task

Instead of a sheet of addition calculations with answers of 10, use a peg board to create the calculations in two colours. A good visual pattern can be created showing the relationships.

Instead of doing some addition calculations with an answer of 100, use the calculator to generate calculations but only using the keys 3, 7, +, – and =.

Instead of doing a sheet of short division calculations, use some cut-out circles and dried peas or counters to physically share out the amounts and then record your findings.

Instead of showing that the angles of a triangle add up to 180°, get the class to draw their own triangles and then get them to measure the angles and compare results.

Working with others

Another dimension of the lesson is the recent increase in England of other adults in the classroom. They are there to support individual's learning, often to ensure a child is included in mainstream education. It is wonderful to have additional help in the classroom but it will need to be managed along with the rest of the curriculum. Does the other adult have the right information to teach the mathematics to that child?

Moving away from the silent classroom of the past, not only the teachers will be communicating but also the children. They will work with the teacher but also with each other. Working in pairs and small groups can be a boost to motivation. It can also allow children to help each other. Again, it is for the teacher to manage these opportunities by ensuring all children gain something from working with others and not always giving or always taking. This adds another management dimension to the lesson but one which is very worthwhile. It is good that not everything has to go through the teacher. Remember those queues at the teacher's desk?

There are many factors which come together to make a good lesson. The role of the teacher is a crucial element in establishing an effective learning environment and it is not easy to get it all right all the time. A well planned and resourced lesson can collapse in a heap when a child spots it is snowing outside! To 'go with the flow' as they say may be the best strategy and then turn it to your advantage. It may not be the planned lesson but use the real life event and its amazing motivational power to capture another piece of learning. Hmm ... can I link some mathematics to snow? It's all about learning.

References

Alexander, R. (ed.) (2010) *Children and their World: Final Report and Recommendations of the Cambridge Primary Review*, Abingdon: Routledge.

Carver, C. (2003) 'Pleasure as a Sign You Can Attend to Something Else: Placing Positive Feelings Within a General Mode of Affect' in *Cognition and Emotions*, 17:2, pp. 241–61.

Green, M. (2013) 'Is Learning Outside the Classroom Worth It?' in M. Sangster (ed.) *Developing Teacher Expertise: Exploring Key Issues in Primary Practice*, London: Bloomsbury, pp. 37–41.

Huckstep, P., Rowland, T. and Thwaites, A. (2003) 'Primary Teachers' Mathematical Content Knowledge: What Does It Look Like in the Classroom?' in *Education-Line* http://www.leeds.ac.uk/educol/documents/00002534.htm (accessed January 2015).

Muijs, D. and Reynolds, D. (2005) *Effective Teaching*, London: Sage.

Pointon, P. and Kershner, R. (2000) 'Making Decisions About Organising the Primary Classroom Environment as a Context for Learning: The Views of Three Experienced Teachers and their Pupils' in *Teaching and Teacher Education*, 16, pp. 117–27.

Price, B. (2013) 'Do Displays Contribute to Children's Learning?' in M. Sangster (ed.) *Developing Teacher Expertise: Exploring Key Issues in Primary Practice*, London: Bloomsbury, pp. 30–3.

Rowland, T., Huckstep, P. and Thwaites, A. (2003) 'The Knowledge Quartet' in *Day Proceedings of the British Society for Research into the Learning of Maths*, Birmingham (November 2003).

Sangster, M. (ed.) (2013) *Developing Teacher Expertise: Exploring Key Issues in Primary Practice*, London: Bloomsbury.

Scoffham, S. and Barnes, J. (2010) 'Happiness Matters: Towards a Pedagogy of Happiness and Well-being' in *Curriculum Journal*, 22:4, pp. 535–48.

Smith, A. and Call, N. (1999) *The ALPS Approach*, Stafford: Network Educational Press Ltd.

Further articles on good learning environments in several subjects can be found in Sangster, M. (ed.) (2013) *Developing Teacher Expertise*, London: Bloomsbury; and Sangster, M. (ed.) (2015) *Challenging Perceptions in Primary Education*, London: Bloomsbury.

16

Teaching Style

When I first started teaching it was normal practice for children to work in silence on individual pages of text books or workbooks. When they finished the page they would bring it out to the front of the classroom where the teacher would mark it and send each child either to do their corrections or move on to the next page. There was an absence of explanation or teaching to the whole class. In fact, there could be a spread of three levels of texts in a single class as those who enjoyed this style of working and could read well sped ahead. Some children, on the other hand, remained on the same book all year.

Desforges and Cockburn (1987) drew attention to the more ridiculous aspects of this way of working when they described two mathematics lessons they had observed. In the first lesson, the children queued to get their page marked. There was a queue on one side for those who had finished the page and another queue on the other side of the teacher's desk for those who had done corrections. As all progress had to be monitored by the teacher, about 80 per cent of the class was queuing at any one time. Explanations to individuals were given occasionally as the teacher marked work from one side then the other. In another school the teacher had observed that there was a lot of queuing in her class so she had set up some mathematics puzzles on the bench alongside the queue to keep them occupied.

I quickly came to notice that certain pages caused great difficulty, often because the explanation was clumsy, the mathematics difficult or the method obscure. It was not long before I used to subvert the system by doing these pages together with the class to get them out of the way. At this stage it had not occurred to me to do the mathematics differently as the whole school was driven by completing the books. In fact, this was my first experience of setting where the able children in my class disappeared to another class for mathematics lessons every day. I have to say, this still left a spread of ability in my lessons.

Hopefully we have moved away from this style of teaching with its absence of communication to the whole class or even groups. Hopefully there is more help for those who are stuck. Hopefully teachers make choices of better ways of teaching particular mathematics rather than leaving it to the author of a book written with no particular children in mind and hopefully children's time on mathematical tasks has increased. To have all children engaged all the time in a class of more than thirty children is not easy and sometimes impossible but a reasonable percentage can be expected with the use of different strategies and styles of teaching.

School structures

Some schools have turned to setting as a solution to the problem of variable progress. Jo Boaler (2000) has much to say about the effects of setting in secondary schools (11 to 16 years). In her study of two English schools, one which set and one which did not, she found that setting advantaged children who enjoyed fast-moving, competitive lessons where there was a pressure to succeed. Set against this was a greater majority who found this environment unhelpful; it made them anxious, the pace felt too fast and they forgot the mathematics. This was particularly true of the girls in these top sets. Furthermore children in lower sets often felt they had been unfairly placed, particularly if their behaviour was poor or they were not 'middle class' and it was hard to move upwards out of a set once they were placed.

These issues did not arise in the school with the mixed ability approach. Most telling was the fact that the exam results did not differ when matched to earlier assessment of ability suggesting that setting made no difference. However, there was one additional factor which may have influenced these findings. The school with the mixed ability approach also encouraged their students to tackle problems by thinking around them and drawing upon the context rather than looking for a cue to apply a learned formula. Boaler saw this as supporting Lave and Wenger's theory of 'situated learning' (1991: 30) as opposed to direct mathematical transfer. This brings our attention back to the style of teaching.

Setting goes in and out of fashion in England. More recently setting has been increasingly used in infant schools (5 to 7 years) as well as junior schools (7 to 11 years), probably to cope with external expectations of pupil achievement. It would be well worth considering if the social and emotional effects of introducing such a system are worth the possible marginal gains in results. Certainly teachers tend to use whole-class teaching when presented with a set but there is always a range of ability even within a set. Beyond lobbying for a change in setting, it is not possible for an individual teacher to change a school system but it is often possible to choose the way you work within your lessons as I discovered with my minor rebellion about the workbook pages!

Key aspects of the lesson chosen by the teacher are how the lesson is structured, what types of groups are used, what style of teaching is used, what tasks are offered and what roles the pupils are encouraged to take on.

Structure of the lesson

The National Numeracy Strategy (DfEE, 1999) in England promoted a distinctive structure for each lesson: a short whole-class mental mathematics section, a teacher exposition section, a pupil working section and a plenary. This has more or less stayed the same since its introduction. As a general pattern it has its merits. An increase in mental calculation and explanations of how to calculate mentally has significantly increased children's mental facility with number and increased their confidence. This talking about 'how it works' is carried through to the teacher's exposition of the day's work. This input to the whole class can be difficult. Whilst there is common ground for all abilities within a topic there will be children who grasp ideas quickly and those who need time to digest new ideas. There is a need to maintain the pace to keep all the class's attention but by using various questioning strategies and levels of difficulty in the examples it is possible to engage the majority of the children.

After a general input children are often divided up into ability groups to tackle aspects of the topic or the same aspect with different amounts of support. This support could be additional equipment or the presence of an adult who will facilitate the learning. Finally the class comes together to share their work or recap on the objectives of the lesson or to pose further questions for future work.

This structure is a long way from the 'open your book and carry on; no talking approach'. There is a role for mental mathematics, explanations, talk and co-operation. It taps into the social context of the classroom and promotes a social constructivist view of how humans learn. Some may argue that there is too much opportunity for copying and this is something the teacher must monitor. However, the advantages of learning from and with each other rather than queuing for the teacher's comments must be considered. Pirie (1991) pointed out that there is the potential for mislearning when peers 'teach' each other but again, with the plenary and more teacher time to support a group of children at any one time, the chances of errors are reduced.

Ways of teaching

There may be national or school directives about the content to be taught and even the structure of the lesson but every teacher teaches differently. Teachers develop their teaching style over time and it is influenced by many factors such as how they were taught themselves, teachers they have observed or worked with, training courses, school expectations and things they have read. They will develop a style they are comfortable with and believe in. It is not easy in time or opportunity to reflect on how they teach but well worth considering whether the way they teach is effective.

How strongly is teaching style based on how children learn? Is style of teaching transferable to different subjects or do children need to experience different ways of working? In a handwriting lesson it might be that the desks are arranged so everyone faces the front and everyone starts by working on the same task. In art there might be a short input and then individuals work on painting their own picture. In mathematics there are times when it is beneficial to work together and other times when group or individual work is appropriate. For example, a lesson on making tangrams might be conducted together and then pairs work out the areas of each shape. A second lesson on subtraction involving practise could be predominantly individual work. The teacher decides the most effective learning approach and draws from a repertoire of strategies. These include different forms of grouping, timing for each task, amount of input, choice of examples, levels of difficulty and degrees of help. Whatever is chosen, the rationale is what is the best learning environment for those particular children?

Style will also include the way a teacher presents a lesson. How much questioning is involved? How fast is the pace of the lesson? Does the teacher give answers early on or ask prompt questions? What type of tasks does he or she give? Does the teacher expect each child to report back after each task or are there some children who can be given several tasks to do before seeing the teacher? How much practise does that child need? Is it possible to give them tasks in problem-solving contexts because they have grasped the mathematics very quickly? Teaching is a complex activity and effective teachers skilfully adjust all of these factors to ensure children have the best learning environment for them.

Task type

Watson and Crick would not have discovered the structure of DNA if they had not been able to build a model of the double helix. The use of equipment to exemplify a situation is invaluable whether you are five years old or fifty years old. Children in English schools have access to a vast number of mathematical resources and most classrooms now have computers, overhead projectors and software which can show the internet and run mathematics programs. Resources are wide ranging but should be used judiciously. As Bentley (2013) points out the computer cannot do the teaching, only support it. It is quite easy to confuse or distract children from the purpose of using it.

There are schools in other countries where successful mathematics is learned but the classrooms are deliberately bare or where resources are non-existent due to poverty. Two students on a teaching visit to Kenya worked in such a classroom (Lever and Newman, 2015). They had thoughtfully taken with them some mathematics resources but found that when they introduced them the children found them strange, got overexcited and confused and were uncomfortable using them. They did not engage with the new resources when they had the opportunity to play. Observing this, the students went away and collected local material such as 'string, sticks, pea pods and sand' (p. 143). It appeared that for the resources to support the mathematical thinking they needed to be familiar and less distracting. One might draw a parallel with the internet in English classrooms. Maintaining a focus on the mathematics is the important point. The resources are there to illustrate and offer another neural link.

The Nuffield Mathematics Project (1964–2004) captured the phrase 'I do and I understand' to illustrate the learning power of practical activities. Although more time consuming, practical tasks are more memorable. They have the advantage of a multi-sensory approach as well as providing another memory hook to aid recall. Most practical tasks are linked to a learning objective, one which needs to be reiterated by the teacher to ensure the underlying principles are grasped. This is done by teacher intervention in the teaching section or in the plenary of a lesson and maybe at the commencement of the next lesson. I am reminded of a stunning but dubious diagram issued by the National Training Laboratories in the USA (accessed 2015). They maintain that the average attention rate for a lecture is 5 per cent, audio-visual presentation 20 per cent, practise by doing 75 per cent and teaching others or the immediate use of learning 95 per cent. If true, case closed!

The quality of the tasks is important too. Does this particular child need lots of practise or can they grasp the mathematics quickly and move to a problem-solving or enquiry situation? Is it appropriate to start with a problem and see what knowledge the child can bring to the situation? Does the child grasp the underpinning mathematics? For example, a worksheet with the calculations shown in the Some sums box can be diligently worked through or, with questioning, a fundamental aspect of mathematics can be revealed.

Some sums

5 + 10 =	7 + 10 =	8 + 10 =	11 + 10 =
15 + 10 =	17 + 10 =	18 + 10 =	21 + 10 =
10 + 5 =	10 + 7 =	10 + 8 =	10 + 11 =
10 + 15 =	10 + 17=	10 + 18 =	10 + 21 =

Maybe I have exaggerated here but does the child realize that adding 10 increases the tens column by 1 and do they realize that 5 + 10 is the same as 10 + 5? This is the key to this worksheet; the mathematics which can be taken away and used again (transfer). This worksheet requires discussion, not just completion. How many tasks exemplify such underlying principles of mathematics and even more important how many children realize the principle?

Some tasks can be used many times and at different levels by tweaking the variables or the amount of given information. For example, to say to a group of children draw an accurate plan of the playground requires decision making about how to go about the task, which parts to measure, what equipment to measure with, what paper to use and what scale to use. A simpler task is to tell children to take the trundle wheel and measure the length and width of the playground. How many decisions does the task require and who will meet the challenge of this task? The more we require children to make decisions, the more independent they will become.

If meaningful contexts aid learning then cross-curricular teaching should help children remember their mathematics. It is important that the context in which the mathematics is used is meaningful and realistic or fun. For example, using graphs to display data which is going to be used such as asking about flavours of ice creams to order for the school fête or which playground games would you like to have? Mathematics can be drawn from story books such as a map drawn of the bear hunt in *We're going on a Bear Hunt* by Rosen and Oxenbury, or the distance of the boy's journey in *The Silver Sword* by Ian Serraillier. Working out the ages of the people buried in the local graveyard or from an extract from the census forms for a history project is purposeful cross-curricular work. If it is a struggle to link mathematics to another subject it is probably best to teach it separately but always be alert to possibilities.

Generally tasks should be relevant to the mathematics principle being learned, be meaningful, realistic if possible and at the least, interesting. If they encourage co-operation and decision making they have the added bonus of supporting independence and social skill development. Over the period of a topic it is good to have a balance of new, do, and solve tasks.

Curriculum requirements may seem as if teaching mathematics will be the same for everyone but even within these bounds there is room for manoeuvre. Effective teachers make many decisions about how they conduct their mathematics lessons, focussing on what is best for each of the children in their class. With large classes compromise will always occur but getting as close as possible to the best learning environment is a worthy goal.

References

Bentley, K. (2013) 'Do Interactive Whiteboards Support or Reduce Creativity in the Classroom' in *Developing Teacher Expertise: Exploring Key Issues in Primary Practice*, M. Sangster (ed.), London: Bloomsbury, pp. 34–6.

Boaler, J. (2000) *Experiencing School Mathematics: Teaching Styles, Sex and Settings*, Buckingham: Open University Press, pp. 125–42.

Department for Education and Employment (DfEE) (1999) *The National Numeracy Strategy Framework for Teaching Mathematics from Reception to Year 6*, London: DfEE.

Desforges, C. and Cockburn, A. (1987) *Understanding the Mathematics Teacher: A Study of Practice in First Schools*, Lewes: The Falmer Press.

Durkin, K. and Shire, B. (eds) (1991) *Language in Mathematical Education: Research and Practice*, Buckingham: Open University Press.

Lave, J. and Wenger, E. (1991) *Situated Learning: Legitimate Peripheral Participation*, New York: Cambridge University Press.

Lever, C. and Newman, C. (2015) 'What Can We Learn from Teaching in a Rural Government School in Kenya?' in *Challenging Perceptions in Primary Education*, M. Sangster (ed.), London: Bloomsbury, pp. 142–7.

The National Training Laboratories, (2015) *The Learning Pyramid* at http://www.learningandteaching.info/learning/myths.htm (accessed January 2015).

The Nuffield Mathematics Project (1964–2004) at http://www.nuffieldfoundation.org/nuffield-primary-mathematics-1964 (accessed January 2015).

Pirie, S. (1991) 'Peer Discussion in the Context of Mathematical Problem Solving' in *Language in Mathematical Education: Research and Practice*, K. Durkin and B. Shire (eds), Buckingham: Open University Press, pp. 143–61.

Sangster, M. (ed.) (2013) *Developing Teacher Expertise: Exploring Issues in Primary Education*, London: Bloomsbury.

Sangster, M. (ed.) (2015) *Challenging Perceptions in Primary Education*, London: Bloomsbury.

17

The Role of Questioning in Enhancing Mathematical Learning

A key aspect of teaching mathematics is the quality of the questions asked by the teacher. Whether it is to elicit information or to prompt thinking, this is a major way to connect with children and build their mathematical understanding. Black et al. (2004) identify questioning as a major part of children's learning and part of the formative process. Questions are a form of scaffolding (Wood et al., 1976), a steering of children's attention towards what is important, a stimulus to their thinking and a way of the teacher understanding the state of a child's knowledge. Torrance and Pryor (1998) see questions as a way of assessing children's knowledge as well as a way to encourage their learning. Questioning is a skill to be developed by the teacher. Effective teachers show a remarkable repertoire of question types which they match well to the needs of the children in their class. They know when it is appropriate to assist and when to challenge.

What types of question could a teacher use? By combining the work of Perrott (1982) and the seminal work of Bloom (1956) a framework can be formed on which to build a range of questions. Perrott (1982) gives an illustrative account of Bloom's classification of teachers' questioning. She expands his six types to indicate how teachers ask them. Here is a summary of Bloom's list alongside Perrott's key words.

Questions which intend to elicit pupil responses:

Bloom (1956)	**Perrott** (1982)	
Knowledge	Who?	Define
	What?	Recall
	Where?	Recognize
	When?	Name
Comprehension	Describe	Put in your own words
	Compare	Explain
	Contrast	
Application	Apply	Employ
	Classify	Give an example
	Use	Choose
Analysis	Why?	What factors?
	Draw conclusions	
	Determine evidence	
Synthesis	Predict	Produce
	Write	Develop
	What would	
	happen if . . .?	
Evaluation	Judge	Assess
	Decide	Justify

Questions

How would you classify the following questions?

What percentage reduction is the sale price of a jacket which originally cost £120 and is now on sale for £96?

Why is the area of a triangle half that of the area of a parallelogram with the same base and the same height?

Which is greater, 1/3 of 15 or 1/4 of 24?

What is the formula for finding the area of a rectangle?

Why is the answer to an even number plus an odd number always odd?

What are the next two numbers in the sequence 2, 4, 8, __, __?

When asked a simple question such as, 'What number comes after 17?' the response will come from a pupil's knowledge base. Either the pupil can recall the factual information or not. This is a lower-order question and only requires straight recall with no expectation to interpret or develop the information or change it in any way from how it was first learned. In mathematics, addition and subtraction facts, multiplication tables and formulae would be likely contexts for lower-order questioning and response.

When a pupil has to alter or use the knowledge they possess to answer a question, the question is categorized as a higher-order question. 'Can you explain how you solved the problem?' would be a typical higher-order question. Interestingly, 'What is 10 take away 7?' might be a higher-order question for a young child if they have to calculate the answer. It turns into a lower-order question for the child once they know the answer is always 3. From this simple example we can see that difficulty is a combination of question type and individual children's knowledge.

A more recent classification of questions specific to mathematics can be found in Jeffcoat et al. (2004). They offer six categories of question types/ prompts:

- Exemplifying, specializing
- Completing, deleting, organizing
- Comparing, sorting, organizing
- Changing, varying, reversing, altering
- Generalizing, conjecturing
- Explaining, justifying, verifying, refuting.

Jeffcoat et al., p. 10

They go on to give examples of appropriate questions for each section and then offer mathematical examples which illustrate each of the types. For example, under 'Changing, varying, reversing, altering' they suggest:

- What do you get if you change . . . ?
- What if . . . ?
- If this is the answer to a similar question, what was the question?
- Do . . . in two (or more) ways.
- What is the quickest, easiest . . . ?

Jeffcoat et al., p. 10

The mathematical examples range from primary school mathematics through secondary school challenges. Two primary level examples for the section above could be: •

How can you change 3 + 4 = 7 into a subtraction?
How can you change a quadrilateral with equal sides into a square?

Jeffcoat et al., p. 18

These are very important questions for mathematical learning as they articulate the underlying relationships that exist in mathematics and promote the thinking that will enable children to function in a mathematical manner. By deliberately extending a repertoire of questions it will follow that children's thinking will be extended and ultimately enable transfer of knowledge to new situations.

It is important that the teacher realizes what kind of question he or she has asked and consequently what kind of response is expected. Does a pupil need time to think? Does the pupil need time to work out an answer? In the example 10 take away 3 the expected response time is going to be different, depending on the knowledge the child holds. Teachers are usually aware of response times needed by individual pupils but sometimes can tend to hurry things along a little too quickly.

Response time is a really important factor when judging the pace of whole-class sessions. If a teacher asks a sequence of higher-order questions to a series of individuals, the pace of the session is going to slow. An example of this would be asking children one after another how they worked out the subtraction calculation on the board. This might be deemed appropriate in situations where there is shared engagement. On another occasion the rest of the children may become disengaged from the teaching and start to find other things to do.

A fast sequence of lower-order questioning will gain a response from many of the class, as long as they already know the information because you are asking them to recall known facts. If a pupil does not know they will not be able to take part. The questioning moves on quickly and there is no time for a 'working out' strategy. Learning for this child is the need to commit to memory a pattern (rote learning). This can be useful when a pattern of facts needs to be learned, such as counting or multiplication tables.

Rowe (1974) researched the effects of 'wait time'. She found that by increasing the time given to answer a question the children began to develop longer answers, children became more confident and non-responses decreased. Children began to respond to each other and more explanations were offered. Generally there was an increase in discourse and encouragingly pupil–pupil discourse developed. Black et al. (2004) included wait time in their research with secondary teachers with positive results. They considered that it allowed students time to think but also raised the expectation of everyone being able to contribute.

The teaching input and plenary could include a mixture of questioning and inclusion strategies. For example: asking the whole class a higher-order question and then targeting a pupil to respond; asking the whole class and then choosing a volunteer; asking one pupil by naming them first; asking everyone to respond together or targeting a group. Add to this higher- and lower-order questioning with expected response times and the teacher can adjust the pace of his or her teaching.

Applying questioning strategies to stages of a lesson

Whole-class introduction of a new learning objective

A brief introduction to the learning objective including a review of links to past work can tune children in to the learning expected. By explaining how the new objective relates to previous mathematics the children can create more neural pathways and in doing so bring past knowledge to support the new objective. Askew et al. (1997) noted the importance of such links when describing the success of their 'connectionist' teachers. This will probably be followed by an expansion of what is to be learned. Both these approaches are an opportunity to draw the children in by using questions which prompt them to recall useful knowledge as well as apply the new knowledge.

Teaching a new learning objective

Whole-class teaching in mathematics lessons is probably one of the most challenging situations in which to function effectively as a teacher. In front of the teacher is a large group of children with a big range of ability, varying knowledge and different speeds of working. As mathematics requires considerable recall and application of facts and skills, pupils are going to vary in their responses. At first this sounds impossible but the class as a whole will be building on knowledge established in previous lessons.

The pace is appropriate when you have the attention and engagement of the whole class. To engage, the pupils need to be able to access the mathematics being offered. This means the work must be pitched at a level appropriate to their understanding. In the whole-class work different levels of work will need to be presented if necessary. This is mainly done through questioning past and present work at various levels of difficulty. For example, when teaching doubling, questions could range from, 'What is double 3?' to 'What is double 37?' The teaching point for everyone is 'doubling', the context of big numbers makes it more challenging for the able pupils and keeps them engaged. For more-able children problem contexts offer more challenging questions and two-step or multi-step calculations can also offer challenge.

Doubling

The teacher introducing the idea of doubling:

Using your white board and working with a partner add 4 and 4. Show me.

Now add 7 and 7. Show me.

How did you work that one out, Alisha and James?

Now add 3 and 3. Show me.

What do you notice that is special about these numbers?

When two numbers the same are added together we call that doubling.

Double 2 and 2. Show me.

Peter, will you double 5 and 5 for us?

Now double 10 and 10. Show me.

I wonder if you can be really clever and double 20 and 20. Show me.

Maria and Hanna, how did you work that one out?

Can you use Maria and Hanna's way to double 40 and 40? Show me.

With your partner make up your own doubling sum.

Now set a challenge for your partner. Give them a number to double but make sure you know the answer.

Take turns and do some more doubling.

(Insert your own style and praise points!)

Group work

In group work the questions become targeted on individuals, probing their understanding and supporting their thinking. For example, 'How did you work that out, Anna?' and 'Ahmed, is there a relationship between this column of numbers and this column?' These are the analytical questions Bloom describes as application, analysis, synthesis and evaluation. You are asking pupils to construct their mathematical understanding. In Piagetian terms this would be described as assimilation and Skemp (1971) called it relational learning. In group work the teacher generates more dialogue and moves between the roles of instructor and facilitator. Through questioning, the teacher has the opportunity to challenge individual children's thinking. It is in this part of the lesson that questions can be pitched most closely to the child's current knowledge.

The plenary

The plenary can take many forms and questioning may play a part. This questioning will probably be at a level where pupils have an opportunity to report back on their learning. For example, 'James, what did you find out when you fitted the cubes in the box?' It might offer some challenging thoughts which open the door for the next lesson. An example after a lesson on area of rectangles might be, 'I wonder if that works for triangles too? You might like to think about that before Friday?'

Finally, there two aspects of using questions that require caution. As Clarke (2001: 87) noted, 'Children typically leave the answering of class questions to the few who appear to be able to respond quickly and are willing to risk making mistakes in public. The teacher can keep a lesson going by questioning in this way, but ultimately knows that the understanding of only a few pupils has been revealed.' More recent strategies to overcome this are the use of individual white boards which are held up with the answer by each child and talk partners which give the children an opportunity to work out solutions through brief peer discussions.

The second pitfall to avoid is the three-stage sequence which turns into a guessing game. As Brissenden (1988) notes, the teacher asks the question, the child gives an answer which is not correct but the teacher immediately moves on to another child and another question without stopping to unpick why the child has given that response. The children soon realize that this is not an environment where it is okay to take risks when responding.

Some of my favourite questions

What happens if we change this . . .? (E.g. length of one side of a triangle.)

When I multiply a number by 6 the answer is 36. What is the number?

How many different ways . . .? (E.g. can you arrange these cubes?)

I don't see how you got that answer. Can you tell me how you did it?

Is it true that . . .? (E.g. there are only two ways to make 5p with coins. Actually there are four ways.)

Why do . . .? (E.g. prime numbers have an odd number of factors.)

Does this always happen? (E.g. when we switch the numbers round in 15% of £12 and 12% of £15) . . . Why?

References

Askew, M., Brown, M., Rhodes, V., Johnson, D. and Wiliam, D. (1997) *Effective Teachers of Numeracy* (final report), London: Kings.

Black, P., Harrison, C., Lee, C., Marshall, B. and Wiliam, D. (2004) *Assessment for Learning: Putting it into Practice*, Maidenhead: Open University Press.

Bloom, B. (1956) *Taxonomy of Educational Objectives*, London: Longman.

Brissenden, T. (1988) *Talking about Mathematics*, Oxford: Blackwell.

Clarke, S. (2001) *Unlocking Formative Assessment*, London: Hodder and Stoughton.

Jeffcoat, M., Jones, M., Mansergh, J., Mason, J., Sewell, H. and Watson, A. (2004) *Primary Questions and Prompts*, Derby: Association of Teachers of Mathematics (ATM).

Perrott, E. (1982) *A Practical Guide to Improving Your Teaching*, Harlow: Longman.

Rowe, M. (1974) 'Wait Time and Rewards as Instructional Variables, their Influence on Language, Logic and Fate Control' in *Journal of Research in Science Teaching*, 11, pp. 81–94.

Skemp, R. (1971) *The Psychology of Learning Mathematics*, Harmondsworth: Penguin.

Torrance, H. and Pryor, J. (1998) *Investigating Formative Assessment*, Maidenhead: Open University Press.

Wood, D., Bruner, J. and Ross, G. (1976) 'The Role of Tutoring in Problem Solving' in *Journal of Child Psychology and Psychiatry*, 17, pp. 89–100.

18

Planning for Progress

Children's progress is the ultimate aim of education but progress in mathematics has always been challenging for some children. The traditional approach of teaching a topic and then assessing it at the end has been under scrutiny for some time now. Torrance and Pryor (1998), Black et al. (2003) and Clarke (2001, 2003) are a few of the people whose notable works promote formative assessment. This is a form of assessment tailored to the needs of the children. By responding more closely in an ongoing fashion to what children understand and have difficulty with, it is felt that better progress in mathematics will be made; not least because children will become more engaged in the subject.

Children's progress and achievement

There is an interesting debate to be had about 'good' teachers. One could argue that a good teacher engages their pupils in the mathematics, the children appreciate the way the teacher works with them and they enjoy their mathematics lessons. This definitely goes a long way to children learning the mathematics as they are likely to remember what they enjoy and there will be a sense of well-being in the lessons. One could also argue that this is good but not enough. Are all the children engaged or just a majority? How does the teacher know that all the children in class are progressing? Will the shy child just 'keep their head down' and let the concepts flow past them? What bits do particular children find difficult or easy? When challenged with such questions there arises a need to find out what each individual can do. A common response to this is to test the children at frequent intervals. The next step of the argument goes; what do you do about the children who did not succeed? Is there time to recap/re-teach those topics? And then, what do you do with the ones who have grasped the mathematics? In some ways this argument cannot be won and it shows us how challenging it is to teach a subject where it is important to ensure knowledge is attained because much future mathematics depends on it. An image comes to mind of a wall with the bricks representing each piece of mathematics understood. As time goes on, some children have constructed rickety walls with missing bricks with an inevitable collapse at a later date, probably sometime in their secondary education.

What is important is that teachers know what each child does understand, where the difficulties lie and have a strategy for resolving them, at the same time providing challenge for those who have a quick grasp of the subject. This is the role that formative assessment has to play for the teacher working day to day in the classroom. Finding out what the children know will also provide feedback to the teacher about the effectiveness of their teaching and what to plan next.

In writing the introduction to this chapter my mind is screaming at me that this process ought to be a dialogue between teacher and pupil and even pupil and pupil and that mathematics as a social learning event has a lot to offer. However, the teacher initiates and controls the lesson within the parameters of national and school expectations and planning and assessing are part of this process.

Long-, medium- and short-term planning

Different countries have different degrees of control over the curriculum. In England the legal curriculum is very detailed and the guidance very strong, even down to the level of how the lesson is structured into three or four parts. In most countries the curriculum is driven by government documents, exam syllabi or a progressive series of textbooks. Whatever the amount of prescription, a systematic approach is important. There was a time in England when children might experience much repetition from year to year or an absence of a topic throughout the school.

To enable progression it is important to have a master plan which works from year to year through the school. This will probably be very similar from country to country because there is a general recognition of how mathematics builds from simple to more complex concepts. If this is a long-term plan, a medium-term plan will also be in place in which the curriculum is divided into terms and within that into units or topics. There are at least two views on the structure of units. The first is to cover a topic in depth once or twice a year. The second is to revisit the topic for shorter periods of time on several occasions, possibly once or twice a term. Those who support the first view think that a longer time studying the topic gives a greater depth of understanding and thus secures the mathematics in children's memory. Those who support the second strategy argue that more frequent 'revisits' to a topic helps children to remember the mathematics as they rehearse it more often. The second strategy can be seen in the weekly 3–2 model where 3 lessons are spent on number work and 2 lessons on another topic such as shape.

The shape of the lesson

Within the lesson itself there are distinct elements which are evident in most primary mathematics lessons. These are the teaching input, children working on consolidating the mathematics, a conclusion or plenary and often a mental mathematics activity. (The mental mathematics has been recognized as a key element of children's facility with mathematics.) The time spent on each of these parts will vary.

The teaching input

There can be some confusion about the key elements of this part of the lesson. This undoubtedly comes from ambiguous vocabulary. The aim of this part of the lesson is to teach the children something new or consolidate what is being worked on. There are several strands which need to be brought together: the objective of the lesson, the mathematics to be learned, the management of class engagement and the instruction of tasks to be completed.

Many teachers favour stating the objective of the lesson at the start. Some teachers write it on the board and others get the children to write it in their books. For young children this can be an unnecessary hurdle and maybe better if addressed briefly and orally. Occasionally it is worth waiting to the end of the lesson and asking the children what the objective was. This can provide an interesting feedback on the effectiveness of the lesson!

The teaching input is crucial. The teacher is the prime resource in the classroom and communicating with the children is seen as key to their learning. This move away from leaving the text book to do the explaining is seen as more effective because the teacher can respond immediately to the children. In this part of the lesson the teacher needs to explain the mathematics clearly. The teacher needs to place the mathematics in context. This could be in a meaningful and familiar situation for the children but also linking it to previously learned mathematics. These connections are more likely to allow the child to make neural connections in their brains; if you like, a form of pegs to hang new learning on to old.

Traditionally, a teacher would offer a 'how to do' model for the children to practise. This is rather like a recipe to be learned. It has been suggested that it is better to include the 'why' or 'how it works' approach. In this way it is hoped that if the children can not recall the 'recipe' they can find other ways to construct a route through to the solution. With more understanding of how the mathematics works, the children can utilize the mathematics in more unfamiliar situations. The teacher can promote this by asking questions, discussing different ways of arriving at the answer and asking children how they worked it out. Children will remember the way which is most meaningful to them. As long as it produces the correct answer it is acceptable and over time more efficient methods can be promoted. Useful strategies in this part of the lesson are to get children to work with a partner or show responses on individual white boards. This allows the teacher to see whether all the children are participating and understanding. Targeted questions at different levels are also more effective than volunteers raising their hands which allows others to opt out.

This part of the lesson needs to be as carefully planned as the activity part as it is where the understanding needs to happen. Good questioning, good models, multi-levelled input and interchange between teacher and pupil and pupil and pupil are the hallmarks of an effective input.

The tasks

The follow-up to the input is when children personally experience the mathematics and consolidate their understanding. If appropriate, a single task might be given to the whole class. For example, tasks such as measuring the area of irregular shapes or finding many ways to calculate an answer of 15. It is more likely that the class will be split into groups if children are working at different levels. For example, different groups might be doing subtraction of hundreds, tens and units, subtraction of tens and units and subtraction of single units from -teen numbers. Further differentiation might take place with the use of resources. One group might have adult input or support throughout. Other groups might have an additional resource such as a number line or number square to aid their memory or, counters to give visual support or, a recording sheet to guide their results.

Plenaries

The plenary is the final part of the lesson. It is usually a short time which can be used in various ways. Usually it is the time when the teacher pulls together the threads of the lesson and reiterates the mathematics which needs to be remembered. This might be done by recapping the learning objectives, by sharing work done by the children, by asking further questions about their learning or, by setting up the next lesson with a question or task. It is important because it is the main learning which should be taken away and remembered by the children.

Within most lessons there is a part called mental mathematics. This is not a mental mathematics test but an opportunity to talk about how to work mathematics out in your head. If this is linked to the mathematics being taught at the time this can make it more powerful. For example, a main lesson on division can be supported by doing a mental input on identifying remainders from known multiplication facts.

The balance of the parts of the lesson depends on the stage reached in that mathematics topic. There may be a longer teacher input in the first lesson, more hands-on work in the next lesson and maybe a longer plenary as the topic draws to a close and the children have an opportunity to share their findings and learning. One of the problems is spending too much time in whole-class mode when children are losing their concentration. This is a judgement call for the teacher.

In planning a lesson what is written down by the teacher depends on what is needed to prompt and clarify. Most of the work has been done beforehand, rather like running a film script, but a script that can be altered if needed as it is delivered. More experienced teachers have 'film scripts' in their head which they tweak and use again depending on the stage and ability of the children in their classes.

Measuring progress

It is possible to teach and not know which children have understood the mathematics. It is possible to deliver the curriculum and wait until a child's understanding is measured at the end of the year or the end of a term. Children's progress is still measured in this way (summative assessment) but think of the lost opportunities to sort out misunderstandings and non-comprehension.

For a more 'fine tuned' approach most teachers adopt formative assessment (Overall and Sangster, 2006). This is the day-to-day monitoring of children's understanding. Why is this necessary? Mathematics is a subject which often builds on previous knowledge so it is important that knowledge is reasonably secure before children move on. If not secure, some children will understand when the topic is next visited; some will not and will find the next dependent piece of mathematics difficult to comprehend. This can go on for years until ultimate failure occurs. Interestingly the group of children who struggle initially but succeed when the next level is tackled show an intriguing aspect of learning. This can be illustrated by those learning to juggle! Juggling with two balls cannot quite be mastered but the person progresses to three ball juggling. This is not mastered either but on return to two ball juggling somehow it now works. This can happen in mathematics and should not be ruled out when making decisions to move on. It also leans in favour of the 'frequent revisit' approach to topics. A good mathematical illustration of this phenomenon can be seen when some children learn to tell the time.

This leads us to a situation where the teacher is monitoring individuals or small groups. What are they seeing?

- Children who have a good grasp of the topic and are ready to be further challenged or move on.
- Children who are nearly there but need a bit more consolidation.
- Children who are struggling to grasp the topic, need diagnosis of the problem and support to learn this mathematics.

Once these observations are made the results indicate what is required next in lesson planning. It is not always appropriate to remain on a topic until all have grasped it, but with good records the teacher will know where to begin next time. This information gathering is aided by a classroom where dialogue about the mathematics takes place. The teacher is the mastermind, planning so that topics in general can be accessed and questions and tasks are pitched at an appropriate level for individual learners.

Creating a classroom where formative assessment can take place

There are some strategies which can be used to support formative assessment in lessons. Creating time within the lesson for monitoring the children is one way. Step back from the teaching for a few moments and watch. Maybe your focus for the lesson is on two of the groups. How are they responding? What evidence is there of understanding? Are children helping each other? Is one child too dependent on another? If there are other adults present they can be used to report back progress with other groups. It is possible to observe small groups but to observe the whole class is not possible in any great depth unless you are looking at written responses.

Written responses and homework require assessment time too. Some of this will be away from the classroom in the form of marking; some will be feedback during the lesson. What is done with homework? Is there time for corrections, time for discussion, time to revisit one or two examples? Maybe there are some short-term targets set about learning in discussion with individual children. When something is wrong it is either a mistake or a misunderstanding. Misunderstandings need time built-in to address them before moving on to another topic. Can this be built into lessons?

Opportunities for discourse have already been mentioned. A further opportunity can be found in the type of task set. Are there decisions to be made in the task? Are there opportunities to work together? Maybe a task can be provided to enable decision making. For example, in this shopping list the items are priced. Which are the cheapest six items? Which would be the most essential items if you could only buy six items? How does this match the cost? Or, can your group design this fairground so that people are likely to spend lots of money?

Questioning forms another element of the formative classroom. When it is the children asking the questions you know that they are fully engaged in the learning. From observation, this is not yet a strong feature of primary mathematics lessons.

In Chapter 4 on independent learners the idea of autonomy is explored and the role the teacher plays in encouraging children's autonomy. Self-assessment could be a part of this process and, besides being an aid to teacher assessment, is a real contribution to children's learning. Children are usually very accurate about their own performance and self-assessment and in the right environment this can lead to self and peer help in tackling difficulties.

In England, there is a great emphasis on record keeping and the need for evidence of pupil progress. There can be much meaningless record keeping. For formative assessment purposes, record keeping is a way of keeping track of children's needs as much as their achievements. The day-to-day informal note taking is going to be the guide to a teacher's lesson planning. Like adults, children forget information so it will be some time before topics are secure and can be utilized in new situations without recent prompts. It might be a whole year before a child spontaneously uses a piece of mathematics to solve a situation. Records at the time are at best tentative in evidencing functional learning. It might be best to turn the assessment around and see it as the beginning of a learning experience rather than the end.

References

Assessment Reform Group (2002) *Assessment for Learning: The 10 Principles*, http://www.ite.org.uk/ite_topics/assessment_for_learning/003.html (accessed February 2015).

Black, P., Harrison, C., Lee, C., Marshall, B. and Wiliam, D. (2003) *Assessment for Learning: Putting it into Practice*, Maidenhead: Open University Press.

Clarke, S. (2001) *Unlocking Formative Assessment*, London: Hodder and Stoughton.

Clarke, S. (2003) *Enriching Feedback in the Primary Classroom*, London: Hodder and Stoughton.

Overall, L. and Sangster, M. (2006) *Assessment: A Practical Guide for Primary Teachers*, London: Continuum.

Torrance, H. and Pryor, J. (1998) *Investigating Formative Assessment*, Maidenhead: Open University Press.

19

Other Factors Influencing the Teaching of Mathematics

There are many factors which influence the teaching of mathematics and this chapter considers just a few of those not covered in previous chapters. These are issues which exist outside the classroom such as government influence, society's expectations and the influence of international practices. A strong feature of this century is the regard paid to international league tables which have become a driver for government decisions. These league tables can affect primary mathematics even when they are test results on secondary students.

National and international league tables

Any league table leads to comparisons either between countries or schools. Inevitably the next step goes beyond performance to what and how mathematics is being taught and asking what the influences on the learning of mathematics might be. The inevitable question becomes, is there a country which has a more effective method of teaching mathematics? And if the answer is yes, can we adopt it in our own country?

The Trends in International Mathematics and Science Study (TIMSS) was initiated in 1995 for eleven-year-olds and ran in 2003 (England: tenth), 2007 (England: seventh), 2011 (England: ninth) and will be conducted again in 2015. These results were better than those for fifteen-year-olds who only appeared in the top ten in 2007 (seventh) and 2011 (tenth). Another international comparison is conducted by the Programme for International Student Assessment (PISA) which was first run by the Organization for Economic Co-operation and Development (OECD) in 2000 and every three years thereafter for fifteen-year-olds. In 2012 the United Kingdom was twenty-sixth out of sixty-five countries in mathematics.

As you can imagine some of the countries were quite upset by the results which were dominated by eastern countries. Baker (1997) describes an early response in America where the media captured the emotive phrase 'Nation at Risk'. Here are some of the proffered reasons for failure. Which of these do you think are valid and how would you respond as a government?

- Education is not valued in this country
- We under spend our competitors on education
- The math and science curriculum is in chaos in this country
- Public schools do not require uniforms
- Students do not participate in janitorial services in school
- There is just too much non-academic fun in U.S. schools
- American students have lower I.Q. scores than Asian children
- Our classrooms are too big; our schools are too big
- Our teachers are under-trained in math and science
- Our teachers are underpaid
- American students do not like math and science
- Our student population is too diverse to teach effectively
- We don't use high-stakes testing to motivate students

Baker, p. 299

The probable effect of these league tables on primary schools in England was the roll out of the National Numeracy Strategy in 1999 from a pilot project in 1995/6. This resulted in improvement in mathematical performance which has now pulled the English primary mathematics results into the top ten but is still not good enough to compete with Hong Kong, Singapore and several other Asian countries. Whilst one might explain away the performance of Hong Kong and Singapore as small nations with more easily managed schools it does not account for places like Japan and Korea. This indicates that the solution is more than a curriculum adjustment. In the intervening years international results has been one of the drivers of research into many other influencing factors such as culture, societal attitudes, motivation, pedagogy, peer pressure, teacher training, teacher knowledge and student well-being; all in an attempt to create more effective mathematics and science education.

The role of government in promoting primary school mathematics

People say mathematics is a universal language and to some extent this is true. Most people agree on the content of mathematics and there is understanding across the world on the mathematics people use. However, there are different approaches to teaching that same mathematics. Factors which influence this variation are: preferred methods, cultural and social expectations, the amount of training and knowledge held by teachers, children's attitude to the subject, the difficulty of the language used to articulate the mathematics and even smaller factors such as class size, use of explanation, time on subject and teacher style.

One cannot underestimate the influence of government decisions. Most governments recognize the importance of the population's understanding of mathematics in its contribution to economic progress. Alongside the learning of English language good mathematical knowledge is going to contribute to the future wealth of the country. As an example, in Malaysia there were a number of years when primary school mathematics and science had to be taught in English to that end. In England a national curriculum was introduced to both schools and teacher training and prescribed numbers of hours required to teach the subject each week. The economic motives of governments cannot be underestimated; they control the numbers and money for schools, for training teachers and for testing students. This is true in many countries and is the parameter within which schools and teachers have to work.

Teacher training

Whilst many countries have curricula which have similar mathematical content, there are considerable variations in how the mathematics is taught, such as the emphasis laid on different calculation methods, application and problem solving. There are variations in the amount of time teachers are trained and particularly in the primary sector, the entry qualifications to that training. For example, students in England will have many different subject qualifications when entering teacher training but all will be expected to teach the majority of subjects and most will teach mathematics lessons.

Students in different countries spend different amounts of time on training. For example, many European countries have a four-year training programme. In contrast in England, if you have a suitable degree and some experience of youth work, you might be able to shorten your training period to six months in the Schools Direct training scheme. This is not common and a postgraduate course is normally one year. Even this leaves little time to address the pedagogy and curriculum content of mathematics education when placed alongside nine other curriculum subjects.

The recruitment of trainees with a range of subject qualifications and the various lengths of training courses must put pressure on students' depth of knowledge to teach mathematics. This has been extensively explored by Liping Ma (2010) in her comparison of American and Chinese primary school teachers. Their personal and pedagogic knowledge for teaching mathematics strongly affected how they presented their mathematics lessons to children. Different countries also wish to convey different philosophical beliefs to their trainees. For example, in Norway trainers lay 'an emphasis on moral purpose' (Stephens et al., 2004: 123). England has a more practical, management approach to its training of teachers.

Cultural and societal expectation

Alongside the governmental framework and sometimes supporting it and sometimes countering it is the influence of culture. Is there an expectation that students will achieve good exam results? Is the country's employment geared to exam achievement? Do parents expect their children to succeed? Do they send their children for additional coaching? Obviously there will be variations in the answers to these questions within any society. In England, the remnants of a class system still haunts parental expectation and even schools to some extent reflect these expectations in their structures such as 11+, grammar schools, secondary modern schools (high schools), free schools and private schools, each with their own set of values. Leung (1998) found education to be highly valued in most East Asian societies and Chen and Stevenson (1995) comment on the expectations of higher mathematical achievement of ethnic Chinese compared with the expectations of Euro-American parents. There is no doubt that societal attitudes are a major influence on student achievement. I was once told of a parent saying to their five-year-old as they entered the school, 'Now, just remember, you don't have to do what they tell you.' Maybe it was a comment made out of context, but alarming all the same.

Parents and siblings are a huge influencing factor, as are peers as children grow older. In a small-scale survey of children in a primary school (Sangster, 2004) I asked who helped them with their mathematics homework. The replies were quite varied: nine children identified someone at home that they could ask for help, eleven nominated helpers, most of whom were parents, siblings, grandparents or friends. Three of the children worked independently. All but one child thought there was someone at home who was good at mathematics. Sometimes it was commented that the parent had declared that he/she was no good at mathematics. This may have been a ruse to avoid the time involved, or a more honest answer, but generally not a good role model for primary school children if it is deemed all right to declare you are not good at something as essential as basic mathematics.

> The empowerment of parents helps children develop their mathematics and view it without anxiety. This enables parents and children to see mathematics as an enjoyable experience, which relates to everyday life. Effective partnership between parents and school is crucial to increasing enjoyment of mathematics for all parties involved.
>
> Fraser and Honeyford, 2000: 91

Parents and schools have a part to play in the motivation of their children. Parents' and schools' attitude to performance and goals will be a strong motivator. This motivation might involve shame, pressure, need for future employment. All are strong extrinsic motivators but the intrinsic motivation of mastery, of interest and pride are probably more sustaining. Self-determination and an ability to work independently are desirable and powerful qualities. Kim et al. (2010) looked at motivational research across different cultures and concluded autonomous motivation has a positive outcome in Asian cultures but this could not be securely generalized across other cultures (Turkey, South Korea, North America and Russia) although it is believed to be so.

The curriculum

There was an occasion when I was given a set of text books from another country and asked to rewrite them for an English market. I did not undertake the task but became aware that countries borrow curricula from other countries. This continues to this day as educators and publishers seek better ways of teaching mathematics. There are some notable adaptations which have had some degree of success in England. Barking and Dagenham, a London Borough, borrowed a curriculum from Switzerland and it ran for a few years in the early 1990s before the National Numeracy Strategy (DfEE, 1999) came into force. What was interesting was the amount of further adaptation the teachers made before it worked with their classes. If you examine the National Numeracy Strategy you will find several methods adopted from the mathematics syllabus of the Netherlands. Real Mathematics Education (Beishuizen et al., 1997) was introduced by the Freudenthal Institute and based its approach on having a problem set in a real situation as a starting point to topics. It also used the empty number line for early calculation and some extended calculation methods. This 'borrowing' nearly always meets with cultural issues. For example, parents find it difficult to assist children with 'new' methods and this can cause tension. The same is true for the teachers who must learn new approaches alien to the way they were taught. Teachers adapt well to new initiatives but it takes time to become familiar and confident with new teaching material.

And then are some things you cannot change. Mathematical language has always been a challenge for some children. In some ways, mathematics is a foreign language. This seems particularly so for the early English learners as they battle with the names of the -teen numbers. By contrast, the logic of the Asian languages may be giving children from these countries a head start. How much easier it is to learn ten-one, ten-two and ten-three than eleven, twelve and thirteen. Ng and Rao (2010) offer a detailed examination of comparisons between American and Chinese number words and mathematical terms and suggest that the Chinese students have an early advantage but they also point out that education is highly valued by Asian parents which probably gives strong external motivation to children learning mathematics.

Social factors

Bourdieu, Bernstein and Wenger are well-known names in the theory of social influence. In mathematics education consideration of this aspect of mathematics education has been and is being explored as we seek ways to make mathematics teaching more effective and learners more successful.

How much do social factors influence performance in mathematics? Kyriakides (2004) examined the effect of socio-economic status on the progress of young children in mathematics in Cyprus. He found that children of lower socio-economic status not only started school at the age of five at a disadvantage but that their progress was slower than children of higher socio-economic status. Why might this be? Brown (2007) proposed that one of the factors was a lack of engagement in discussion by these children. Rather like second language learners, if the child is alienated from the 'community of practice' (Lave and Wenger, 1991) they are not joining the discourse or co-constructing knowledge. Brown suggests that it is the teacher who must create the community by listening, observing, questioning, challenging, drawing out connections and asking for explanation and justification. The more the teacher takes a facilitator role the more children will be drawn in to the community.

Another factor might be the way children with lower socio-economic status perform on assessments; particularly those with mathematics problems in real contexts. According to Cooper and Dunne (1998) test questions loaded with socio-cultural meaning are not always understood mathematically by lower status children. They found that on the eleven-year-old national tests of 1992 there was a tendency for them to respond in a practical, real life way and not realize it is just a context for a piece of pure mathematics. Schuchart et al. (2015) examined children in Germany and found a similar but less marked response. But they, like Brown, recognized the importance of the role of the teacher in creating an inclusive and effective environment.

The teacher has a big role to play in promoting equal opportunity and with an awareness of the difficulties which might arise when doing problem solving and talking mathematics (Lubienski, 2000). Children can be encouraged to engage and verbally express their ideas and explanations.

Finally, a factor which schools and teachers are very aware of is the role the home has to play in encouraging mathematics learning. Whether it is parents, grannies or siblings who are willing to support children, how best do teachers utilize this further and valuable resource?

References

Baker, D. (1997) 'Surviving TIMSS: Or, Everything You Blissfully Forgot About International Comparisons' in *The Phi Delta Kappan*, 79:4, pp. 295–300.

Beishuizen, M., Gravemeijer, K. and Van Lieshout, E. (eds) (1997) *The Role of Contexts and Models in the Development of Mathematical Strategies and Procedures*, Utrecht: Freudenthal Institute.

Brown, R. (2007) 'Exploring the Social Positions that Students Construct Within a Classroom Community of Practice' in *International Journal of Educational Research*, 46, pp. 116–28.

Chen, C. and Stevenson, H. (1995) 'Motivation and Mathematics Achievement: A Comparative Study of Asian-American, Caucasian-American, and East Asian High School Students' in *Child Development*, 66 (pp. 1215–34) cited in S. Ng and N. Rao (2010) 'Chinese Number Words, Culture, and Mathematics Learning' in *Review of Educational Research*, 80:2 (June 2010), pp. 180–206.

Cooper, B. and Dunne, M. (1998) 'Anyone for Tennis? Social Class Differences in Children's Responses to National Curriculum Mathematics' in *Sociological Review*, 46:1, pp. 115–48.

Department for Education and Employment (DfEE) (1999) *The National Numeracy Strategy Framework for Teaching Mathematics from Reception to Year 6*, London: DfEE.

Fraser, H. and Honeyford, G. (2000) *Children, Parents and Teachers Enjoying Numeracy*, London: David Fulton.

Kim, J., Kim, M. and Schallert, D. (2010) 'An Integrative Cultural View of Achievement Motivation: Parental and Classroom Predictors of Children's Goal Orientations when Learning Mathematics in Korea' in *Journal of Educational Psychology*, 102:2, pp. 418–37.

Kyriakides, L. (2004) 'Differential School Effectiveness in Relation to Sex and Social Class: Some Implications for Policy Evaluation' in *Educational Research and Evaluation*, 10:2, pp. 141–61.

Lave, J. and Wenger, E. (1991) *Situated Learning: Legitimate Peripheral Participation*, Cambridge: Cambridge University Press.

Leung, F. (1998) 'The Implications of Confucianism for Education Today' in *Journal of Thought* (pp. 25–36), cited in S. Ng and N. Rao (2010) 'Chinese Number Words, Culture, and Mathematics Learning' in *Review of Educational Research*, 80:2 (June 2010), pp. 180–206.

Lubienski, S. (2000) 'Problem Solving as a Means Toward Mathematics for All: An Exploratory Look Through a Class Lens' in *Journal of Research in Mathematics Education*, 31:4 (pp. 454–82) cited in C. Schuchart, S. Buch and S. Piel (2015) 'Characteristics of Mathematical Tasks and Social Class-related Achievement Differences Among Primary School Children' in *International Journal of Educational Research*, 70, pp. 1–15.

Ma, L. (2010) *Knowing and Teaching Elementary Mathematics*, Abingdon: Routledge.

Ng, S. and Rao, N. (2010) 'Chinese Number Words, Culture, and Mathematics Learning' in *Review of Educational Research*, 80:2 (June 2010), pp. 180–206.

PISA information can be found at http://en.wikipedia.org/wiki/Programme_for_International_Student_Assessment (accessed January 2015).

Sangster, M. (2004) 'Parents and Mathematics in the Primary School' in *Proceedings of the British Society for Research into Learning Mathematics (BSRLM)*, 24:2 (June 2004).

Schuchart, C., Buch, S. and Piel, S. (2015) 'Characteristics of Mathematical Tasks and Social Class-related Achievement Differences Among Primary School Children' in *International Journal of Educational Research* 70, pp. 1–15.

Stephens, P., Tonnessen, F. and Kyriacou, C. (2004) 'Teacher Training and Teacher Education in England and Norway: A Comparative Study of Policy Goals' in *Comparative Education*, 40:1, pp. 109–30.

TIMSS information can be found at http://en.wikipedia.org/wiki/Trends_in_International_Mathematics_and_Science_Study (accessed January 2015).

20

A Teacher's Voice

It is hard to capture the essence of a classroom where effective learning is taking place. Success is a mixture of so many elements. These elements can come together just for a lesson or for more sustained periods of time and the teacher knows when it is all working. Every teacher strives to capture those moments as they are rewarding for the children as well as the teacher.

It is for each teacher to interpret and move within the framework of expectations and requirements. Each teacher is precious and unique. They can put their own spin on how they teach mathematics. The more meaningful the mathematics is for the children, the more effective the teacher will be in engaging them in learning. Sometimes the elements are obvious such as the curriculum content, stimulating activities, the planning and the tracking of progress. Other elements are more subtle such as the creating of an empathetic environment where every child can voice a view about their mathematics. It is certainly embedded in the decisions teachers make about all aspects of their teaching.

> Within their classrooms, effective teachers create learning environments which foster pupil progress by deploying their teaching skills as well as a wide range of professional characteristics. Outstanding teachers create an excellent classroom climate and achieve superior pupil progress largely by displaying more professional characteristics at higher levels of sophistication within a very structured learning environment.
>
> DfEE, 1.1.9, 2000

Here is a series of extracts from a small–scale research project in a classroom of a teacher (C) who strongly valued creating independent learners of her ten- and eleven-year-olds. Hopefully it gives a little insight into the teacher's voice in such a classroom.

- 'There were times when we as teachers expect children to operate independently and there are times when we wish to teach them to work in that style. This second mode looks very directed but the purpose is to develop skills and encourage thinking which they will then be able to use on their own. In the classroom the teacher is moving back and forth between these modes with the whole class and with individuals who will display varying degrees of independence. The important factor is that the teacher at all times is aiming at developing independence in the class group and in individuals.'

- 'You've got those who can do it naturally and those who, even though they are Year Six (age eleven), don't like to be away from you because they lack confidence. You have to plan for and build up strategies for those children. They are continually coming back for support so you have to work especially with those children, saying, "I don't want you to come back into the classroom for fifteen minutes," so that they get used to being away from you.' (C has a workspace just outside her classroom linked to the room by a large archway. This is referred to as 'outside'.)

- C says, 'The [independent] child will question and want to discuss things and that will create problems with discipline. You begin to wonder, "Am I in control of these children or are they in control of me?" That's all part of the independent person. They will question, "For what reason are you asking me to do this?" This is why establishing a good relationship with the children is so important.' C admitted she liked control as a teacher but not the control she used to establish. 'With these children it is a more co-operative situation; more, "If you scratch my back, I'll scratch yours". We sort of co-habit.'

- Is independence about letting go then? 'Yes, it's like having a child and them wanting to go to their first disco. You've got to be prepared to let them go without you. You've got to be willing to let go. The teachers know which children they can trust and get good work from and then you have to feed the others in and let them have a chance. If the child makes a mess of the chance you find another opportunity for them. That can go on all year with some children.'

- She has some lovely humorous and illuminative phrases such as, 'If in doubt look it up. The books are on the bookshelf. Don't look it up in my brain.' Alongside these comments to the class she quietly talks to individuals about interests and things they need help with. She is so well organized she knows exactly what work each child is doing (information kept in a large hardbacked book). The impression she gave was she was aware of all the children all the time! Her previous class who had been with her a year needed very little instruction and were involved in longer projects and changed tasks without direct teacher input.

Armed with the knowledge about how children learn and good ways to teach mathematics, the rest is about how a teacher chooses to teach within the set expectations of the environment in which they are working. Teachers' choices are based on their beliefs and understanding of the mathematics and how children learn the mathematics. What are your choices on how to teach mathematics?

Always, it is worth reflecting on one's own practice. It might be that you confirm your own teaching strategies or it prompts you to try something different. Even small changes can contribute to more effective learning. If this book means that you do change one thing, then it has been worth it.

Reference

Department for Education and Employment (DfEE) (2000) *Researching into Teacher Effectiveness: A Model of Teacher Effectiveness*, Report by Hay McBer to the DfEE.

Index